BEGINNING

YOUR MARRIAGE

EIGHTH EDITION

by
John L. Thomas, S.J.

revised by
David M. Thomas

ACTA Publications
Chicago, Illinois

Beginning Your Marriage, 8th Edition
by John L. Thomas, S.J., Ph.D.
revised by David M. Thomas, Ph.D.

NIHIL OBSTAT
The Rev. Edward L. Maginnis, S.J.
Censor Deputatus

IMPRIMATUR
+ The Very Reverend Donald F. Dunn
Vicar General for the Diocese of Colorado Springs
April 29, 1994

Our thanks to Mary Buckley, William Urbine, David Fortier, and several family life ministers in various dioceses around the country, all of whom contributed insights and suggestions for this edition.

Edited by Gregory F. Augustine Pierce
Artwork by Isz
Typeset by Garrison Publications

Excerpt from *Precious Jewel Person* by Barbara Ritter Garrison on page 29 used with permission of ACTA Publications. Excerpt from *The Velveteen Rabbit* by Margery Williams on page 46 used with permission of Doubleday & Co., Inc.

Copyright © 1994:   ACTA Publications
"Assisting Christians To Act"
4848 N. Clark Street
Chicago, IL 60640
312-271-1030

Library of Congress catalog number: 94-070380
ISBN: 0-915388-24-3
Printed in the United States of America

DEDICATION

This mutual inward moulding of husband and wife, this determined effort to perfect each other, can in a very real sense . . . be said to be the chief reason and purpose of matrimony . . . .

Pope Pius XI

These words—written in 1930—show that the Church has long been concerned about the quality of the relationship between husband and wife, which is the basis for a good and holy marriage and the foundation of a strong family.

The need to prepare for marriage carefully and intelligently has never been so urgent as it is today. We are challenged constantly by the joys and sorrows of the modern world, and it is no small feat for marriage and the family to meet these challenges.

Marriage is the intimate and ultimate responsibility of the two people who choose to embark upon this wonderful, yet solemn, adventure together.

It is to this responsibility and to you who willingly assume it and share in fostering the nobility of marriage and the family that *Beginning Your Marriage* is dedicated.

INTRODUCTION TO THE
EIGHTH EDITION

I was honored to be chosen to revise this classic book. Father John L. Thomas, S.J., who died in 1991, was a true pioneer in the Catholic Church of the United States. He was among the first to combine the findings of behavioral science, especially sociology, with the insights of Catholic theology. He chose the areas of marriage and the family as his primary scholarly focus. Not content with just the world of scholarship, however, Father Thomas involved himself in assisting countless couples in preparing for their marriages. From these experiences came *Beginning Your Marriage.*

I recall my first meeting early in my own career with this priest-scholar, with whose works I was already quite familiar. I was delighted that he had also heard of me. His ethnic background was Welsh, where Thomas is a common last name. He was certain that we were distant relatives, especially because my first name was David. St. David is the patron saint of Wales. Unfortunately, I had to disappoint him because my ethnic roots stem from Lithuania and Germany. Like that of many sons and grandsons of immigrants, my last name was altered to appear more American. Nevertheless, this meeting initiated a friendship that lasted until his death. In fact, his original hopes proved partially correct. We eventually saw ourselves as brothers "of a sort." We shared a healthy humor about things human and ecclesial. We knew that God's most important concerns were for ordinary people, like him and me.

What we did not share were our sacramental identities. John was an ordained Jesuit. I am a married lay person. My wife, Karen, and I have been married twenty-eight years, and we have been blessed (on the good days) with five children who now all tower over their mother. We have also had the privilege of providing foster care for over seventy of God's precious little ones.

I earned my doctorate in theology from the University of Notre Dame in 1971. For most of my academic career, I directed my attention to Christian marriage and family life. I was a *peritus* (consultant) to the United States bishops' delegation to the World Synod on Family Life in Rome in 1980. Soon after that, I founded a graduate program in family ministry and adult religious education at Regis University in Denver, Colorado. The program expanded over the years and now operates under the broader concept of community leadership. Family life remains, however, at the heart of our program.

What I have tried to do in this revision is to update some of Father Thomas' insights to more effectively meet the concerns and questions of couples beginning their marriage today. I have expanded the sections dealing with responsible family planning, infertility, two-income marriages and blended families. More discussion is also offered on interethnic and interfaith marriages. I have tried to remain true to the voice and spirit of Father Thomas, while adding some of my own ideas that flow from my experiences as another kind of "father" Thomas. May our book continue to help couples develop wonderfully satisfying marriages in a time when no one claims it is easy.

David M. Thomas

CONTENTS

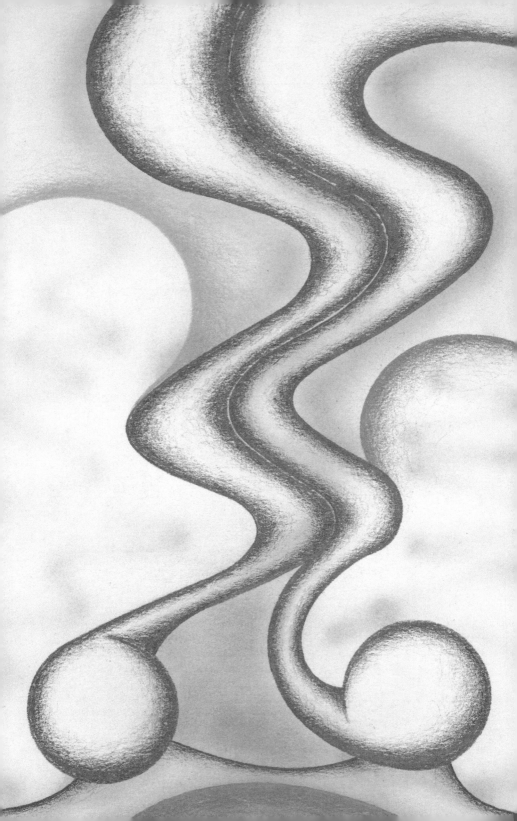

CHALLENGE OF COMMITMENT

Marriage is a radical new way of life that can be wonderful, exciting, fulfilling, and sometimes frightening. You should both be proud, happy, hopeful, and a little scared as you enter it.

It is certainly all right to feel a bit apprehensive about your future together. This shows that you already grasp some of the awesome responsibilities that lie ahead of you. After all, you are about to embark on one of the most important journeys of your life. If you took this lightly, that would be cause for concern. Moving ahead with a lump in your throat and wobbly knees is a good sign.

It is also a good sign if you feel that you might have something more to learn about marriage. We hope that this book will provide you with some ideas worth thinking about and some questions worth asking.

INTERDEPENDENCE

When you marry, you give up something and you gain something. You lose some of your independence and you acquire the attitudes and lifestyle of *interdependence*. During adolescence and young adulthood, you struggled mightily to achieve the ability to stand on your own. Good for you. Gaining independence is no small achievement.

Some people are surprised to learn that independence is an important foundation for marriage. When two mature, independent people marry, they bring their separate vigor and muscle into marriage. They form a relationship of rich interdependence, one that accentuates each partner's strengths and supplements any weaknesses.

We hope that description will apply to you. You are just at the point of beginning the challenging task of creating an interpersonal structure of interdependence. You can do this because the two of you are freely and joyfully choosing to join your lives, to marry with deep love for each other. You no longer want to live life as a soloist, you desire to become one half of a duet.

As a single person, the center of your life was you. After you fell in love, your personal center expanded to include another person. Wonderful feelings accompanied the experience of falling in love. And marriage became the logical step as the two of you decided to share your lives permanently. You became willing to exchange the freedom you experienced as an independent single person for a new kind of freedom, an interpersonal freedom, which will become a rich treasure, shared in common, as you live out your married life.

In one sense, the decision to marry is not strange or unusual. Most adults make the same choice. Sociological surveys continue to tell us that the desire for a happy marriage and family life stands at the top of almost everyone's list of hopes and dreams. Even with the high divorce rate, marriage is still chosen by the vast majority of adults.

New trends also indicate that people are marrying later in life. Second marriages after the death of a spouse or after a divorce are also on the rise. These are very important alterations to long-standing social patterns.

Of course, the large numbers of married folk tell only part of the story. You may correctly ask, "Are married people today really happy? In giving up independence for interdependence, do most people really experience greater joy and satisfaction in their lives?"

In general, it seems that they do. But everyone recognizes happiness is not the lot of all married couples. The number of divorces granted each year is almost one-half the number of marriages begun that same year. That doesn't shape up as a very hopeful scenario.

But think about it. It can also be argued at least half the marriages today are quite happy. Never before in human history has it been easier to walk away from an unhappy marriage. Yet the majority of couples choose to stay together. And what's even more important for you to know as you plan your own marriage is this: You can take positive steps now to insure that *your* marriage will be listed among those described as happy, harmonious and healthy.

Therefore, the statistics of failure need not paralyze you. In fact, you probably know many couples who are living married lives of happiness and fulfillment. The trick is to find out what makes their marriages work and to recreate—*in your own way*—their success stories.

CREATIVE LOVE

Loving means summoning forth another with the loudest, most insistent call. Loving means stirring up in the beloved a sometimes mute and hidden being who can't help leaping at the sound of your voice.

Love calls forth life. Love brings forth wonderful aspects of oneself and of the other. From Claudia, for example, Brian gets a vision of what she wants him to be, believes him to be, and what he might really become. With the security and inspiration of Claudia's love, Brian dares to change, to strive to become his best self. He may put aside fears, become more sensitive, find the courage to take risks, and become motivated to use the talents he possesses. In pursuing the vision of himself revealed by Claudia's love, Brian grows. It is as if, in the fire of love, there is a spark which ignites what's best in each person. Love can truly be transforming.

Each partner brings certain strengths and weaknesses to a marriage, as well as a great potential for success or failure. Married love can and should bring forth the best qualities in both partners. Claudia knows that, although Brian has seen the worst side of her personality on many occasions, he still loves her. She can become more secure and accepting of herself and can get to the business of being real. She need not "play games" with Brian. Being secure in the love of another is among life's greatest blessings.

Most couples marry while deeply in love, and they plan to remain so. Yet a tragic number of "once-in-love" couples lose that precious feeling. Once again, it doesn't have to be that way. Marriage, blessed and enriched by God, remains a very human relationship. It is built on freedom and remains strong when each marriage partner makes wise choices not only about whom to marry but on what to do after the wedding.

It may be obvious, but when you think about it, marriages fail for only one of two reasons. Either you marry the wrong person, or you marry the right person but fail to do the right things once married.

Listen to this young man who was overheard while waiting in line for a marriage license. "It seems kind of silly to be getting a license now that the hunt is over." This unfortunate groom-to-be didn't seem to realize that falling in love and celebrating a beautiful wedding is no guarantee of "living happily ever after." Maybe it would be better if he were humming, "We've only just begun."

WORKING AT LOVE

So why do so many couples end up in the divorce court? A number of reasons are offered: false expectations about what marriage is really like, immaturity on the part of one or both partners, excessive stresses generated by today's social and economic systems, and self-centeredness which renders some couples incapable of making the compromises and adjustments necessary in healthy marriages. This is a mixed bag indeed! And these explanations, taken individually or in deadly combination with each other, may still not tell the total truth. In fact, they can prevent us from noticing what's really at the heart of marital success: the growth of love.

At first glance, this may appear as almost simplistic. After all, are not most couples *completely* in love at the time of their wedding? The answer is both yes and no.

It is important to remember that love is not simply a feeling or emotion. At the time of the wedding, couples may experience the feeling of love at what seems to be its maximum. But love is more than an emotional state. It is related to every aspect or part of the total person. It is thoughts, words and deeds—as well as feelings. And while love may seem to exist primarily *in* a person, it is really something *between* persons. If you look at love that way, it is easy to imagine that there are really no boundaries for genuine love. Its growth can be without limit.

When marriages succeed, they are always in search of "more." The joyful, exhilarating experience of early love is important, necessary and delightful. But falling in love is a beginning of something great, not its culmination. Love must be carefully nurtured, fostered, "worked at" by both partners throughout the marriage. Let's face it, it is easy to maintain a loving relationship during courtship, when both partners tend to be on their best behavior. Agreements and concessions regarding the future are easily made because they cost so very little then. As one young wife, accused by her husband of not living up to some of the promises she had made before marriage, responded, "But John, dear, those were only campaign promises!"

INESCAPABLE INTIMACY

One of the first challenges to your love early in marriage is being faced with inescapable intimacy between two somewhat imperfect, limited persons. Each one of you carries into your marriage a certain amount of baggage called "your past life." Since everyone is influenced by a different past, each of you experience a slightly different present. Further, it is impossible for both of you to share exactly the same dream for the future.

For example, each of you comes from a different "family of origin"—the family in which you were raised. No matter how similar you might think your backgrounds are, there are always wide variations in how your families of origin operated. One family might have encouraged its members to express feelings and discuss problems openly, for example, while the other may have "let sleeping dogs lie." Your "birth order" also has influenced how you see and react to things. An eldest and a youngest child will often react to situations very differently, as will an only child and a member of a large family.

Another source of differences may be the fact that one of you is male and the other female. While the debate over the exact nature and extent of gender differences will be around for a long time, some observations are worth mentioning. For instance, it seems men tend to value their careers and successes outside the home setting more than women do. Women, on the other hand, appear to be more sensitive to relationships which center around the home. Men appear more goal-oriented and women more process-oriented. Men like arrivals, women enjoy the trip. Men attend more to factual information, women enjoy stories. It is important not to think any of these differences are set in stone. In fact, in your relationship the situation might be just the opposite on any of these points. Still, there will be differences between you.

The task of marriage is to bring two very different people together in a new unit (called a family) with its own traditions and ways of operating. The key to the successful accomplishment of this task is the development of *intimacy* between a husband and a wife. Intimacy is not an attempt to deny or gloss over differences. It is, rather, the willingness and ability to get behind or underneath these surface or superficial differences to the real person. Married couples are intimate with each other in ways that are impossible in any other kind of relationship.

Although marital intimacy can and usually does offer a deep measure of personal happiness, it can also bring couples face to face with real challenge. The sacred promise and commitment made on the wedding day before God, family and friends is open-ended. You pledge to live into the future with each other for the rest of your lives, sharing both joy and sorrow, success and failure. Needless to say, no one knows the future. The traditional words expressing this open-endedness are familiar: "I take you for better or worse, for richer or poorer, in sickness and in health, until death do us part." This is a beautiful promise and, while idealistic, it can be done. Countless average, ordinary married couples have done this before you. They all learned that it takes a special kind of love to achieve the intimacy that makes a successful marriage. You know something about this special love right now. As the days unfold, you will learn a lot more and can grow into its invitation to a fuller life.

FIRST YEARS OF MARRIAGE

The first years of marriage, most couples will tell you, are the most challenging. It is a time when you "fill in the blanks" about each other. Full knowledge of your spouse requires the actual experience of day-to-day married life. Some expectations of each other will have to be adjusted. You will, no doubt, have a surprise or two. The routine of daily life sometimes erodes romantic enthusiasm. And you will both have to learn to deal with misunderstandings of each other's desires and gestures. This kind of understanding of another cannot be learned by simply "living together." Knowing it's "for keeps" deepens everything.

Recall that healthy marriages are built on interdependency. Two people enter a marriage and build their marriage by freely giving to each other love, care and concern. The early stage of marriage is the time for learning to mesh two sets of freedoms, lest the couple end up simply as "married singles" who merely live their lives side-by-side in peaceful coexistence. Only committed, intimate love will give you the courage and strength and motivation to take those steps necessary to become true partners for life.

It is unwise to underestimate the difficulties and challenges of the early years of marriage. Interpersonal patterns are established almost right away, and they can either build up or break down the marriage right from the start. In those marriages which break up in their early years, what is sad is not so much that "things didn't work out" but rather that the couple never really gave the marriage a chance.

MYSTERY OF LOVE

The word "love" seems to have as many meanings as do the number of people who use the word. That's an exaggeration, but love is one of those words that can describe many different feelings, attitudes and actions. Even the human sciences like psychology and philosophy offer widely different descriptions of this state. In fact, those who like to employ a strict scientific method to what they describe consider love almost nonexistent, since it cannot be readily measured, predicted or controlled. Even the ancients like King Solomon had to admit frankly that they couldn't understand "the way of a man with a maid." Perhaps Solomon was a bit confused himself, since it is reported that he had over "seven hundred wives of royal rank, and three hundred concubines."

Love between a woman and a man may be aptly described as a mystery. Haven't you ever overheard at a wedding, "I wonder what Jack sees in her?" or "Whatever in the world can a girl like Jill see in him?" While such remarks may often be tarnished by jealousy, they also illustrate the incomprehensibility of love.

Of course, there is another meaning of mystery, which is that the reality is so deep, profound and spiritual that it cannot be reduced to simple definitions. There always seems to be more there than can be comprehended. That is exactly what genuine love is. It is a mystery to those who experience it, and it is a mystery to those who observe it. It is no wonder that many conclude that such a powerful force in the universe must be divine.

Nevertheless, we can describe some of the characteristics of love between a man and a woman. It is a strong, affective, emotional attachment having aspects of sexual attraction, desire and tenderness. It is an attitude which desires what is best for the beloved. It is the force that initiates marriages and keeps them growing for decades and decades.

LOVE IN MARRIAGE

We learn about the meaning of love in marriage from a variety of sources. We have observed it in our families of origin. We view it in movies and on television. We read about it in novels and short stories. In the distant past, when most marriages were arranged by parents, romantic love before marriage was almost unheard of. What's ironic is that today if one is not in love when marrying it is considered totally inappropriate. How times have changed!

True love involves a reorientation of one's person and one's lifestyle. The beloved becomes a new focal point of attention and desire. It is as if life now has two centers, you and your partner. While this can be confusing and make life much more complicated, it remains a wonderful way to live. That is why so many couples still make marriage their ultimate "lifestyle" of choice.

INFATUATION

Mature love, however, is very different from infatuation. Unfortunately, too many people under the spell of infatuated attraction commit to marry. In reality, they are not really in love with another person, although it may seem that way. They are more in love with the feeling of warmth and excitement which is associated with the thought or the presence of the "beloved." You might have heard the phrase "love is blind." This is a characteristic of infatuation.

While a person is under its influence, the other person is placed in a radiant light. Their good personal traits are amplified. Their faults are ignored. The beloved appears to possess the beauty and personality of a movie star, the intelligence of a research scientist, and the resources of a millionaire. The very thing which is dangerous (and delightful) about infatuation is the fantasy. Its emotion is ecstacy and its belief is perfection. A great deal of the popular music of love is filled with the language of infatuation.

Real love between a woman and man includes two separate desires: the desire to love the other and the desire to be loved by the other. The one is other-centered and the second is self-centered. Infatuation feeds more on the need to be loved than on that of actively loving another. Deep, mature love is, on the other hand, the blend of the two desires. It is mutual and interdependent. One word of caution, however, needs to be mentioned. It is both dangerous and impossible to try to calculate this "balance." Such calculation is too fallible, too misleading, and can create a tug of war rather than a sharing of life. As the saying goes, marriage is not a fifty-fifty arrangement. It is more like a one hundred percent deal.

Infatuation is a common phase of most loving relationships, particularly when there is a strong sexual attraction. Infatuation is not bad. In fact, it can be argued that, like all love, its source is God's loving presence in our lives. Just remember that it is an early stage of your love together. Yet it is important because it did stop you in your tracks to take a second look, a look that will last a lifetime!

LOVE INVESTMENT

Here is a common form of advice given to married couples: Learn to express your love to your spouse in a thousand different ways. It's an adaptation of Elizabeth Barrett Browning's poetic reflection: "How do I love thee? Let me count the ways."

The ways of expressing love are amazingly varied. They can differ with age and sex, with personality and culture. What cuts across all of them is that each expression embodies concern and care for the other person. Expressions of love are cumulative. They add up over the days and years to form the treasured marriage all desire. The goal of this love investment is to create a new level of intimacy, a human relationship which is not possible in any other form save marriage.

A love investment includes an intellectual dimension. Ideas and beliefs are shared which builds up both partners' understanding of themselves and the world around them. Marriage is like a school of love and intimacy. Hopes and dreams are shared. We learn to see the world through the other's eyes, as well as our own. To accomplish this growth in understanding requires an open mind and a valuing of the other's perceptions and interpretations. This is a great challenge because each person tends to defend his or her own view of things.

Another dimension of the love investment is emotional and psychological. Spouses grow to care deeply about each other and to support each other's deepest psychological needs. Married couples often become "best friends," who know each other's worst fears and weaknesses, who share each other's greatest joys and sorrows, and who are "there" for each other whenever needed. The nakedness that married couples share during lovemaking is symbolic of their emotional and psychological closeness.

A love investment also has material and physical dimensions. These involve the use of common goods and common space. Maturing love will include sharing and generosity, as well as an increase of tenderness and sensitivity to each other's physical and material desires. There will be a willingness to give and receive joy and pleasure on all levels.

Finally, a love investment has moral and spiritual dimensions. True love includes the desire to promote and assist one's marriage partner in becoming a more complete person. This includes not only sensual gratification but also spiritual growth, which includes each one's relationship to God. At this deepest level of the sacred, husband and wife encounter the deepest meaning of their love.

PROCREATION

Only couples willing to make a "love investment" can be said to truly love each other. That investment can also pay big dividends in the desire to have children.

Wanting a child or children is a very complex issue. It can be based on biological, psychological and social reasons. But deep down, the desire for children can ideally be traced to a strong spiritual foundation. From a belief in God as the author of life, and from a wish to cooperate with God in bringing new life into the world, couples choose to expand their love in the service of new life.

It must be mentioned that some of the many reasons for wanting to have a baby are neither loving nor generous. To have a child simply because one desires to call someone "my own" or "ours" can be self-centered and immature. Procreating should not be done to prove one's masculinity or femininity or to insure a piece of immortality. Nor should it be done simply to please or impress others, for example parents.

A healthy and holy procreative desire is the result of the love of two mature people and their decision to embody their love for each other in the life of another. By having a child, the couple extends themselves in a new way. Their love expands to the next generation of human beings.

For those couples who cannot have children, the love investment will result in the desire to be generous and outgoing. Many options stand before the childless couple: adoption, foster care and a whole host of other possibilities to "be fruitful and multilply." However procreation occurs in marriage, it is the couple's special way of announcing that their love is so great that it cannot be contained in themselves but must be shared with others.

CHRISTIAN VOCATION

Each Christian is invited to respond in the ordinary activities of life as an embodiment of God's love. Jesus' two great commandments, love of God and love of neighbor, are integral. We express our love of God, who is love, through our love of others. Christians understand their lives as more than simply blending one day into the next and the next. Christians are called to help bring about the reign of God now, in their daily lives.

When the word "vocation" is used, it more often than not implies the vocation to priesthood or religious life. Throughout the centuries, becoming a priest, sister or brother were understood as special ways in which Christians followed Jesus.

What is exciting about the time we live in, however, is the growing appreciation of the fact that there are many more Christian vocations than just those. Lay people in the world also are called by God to a special vocation. This new understanding of vocation, described at the Second Vatican Council, includes living "in" the world and living "for" the world. It is characterized by "getting mixed up with" seemingly worldly things like jobs and technological inventions and different people in all kinds of ways. It definitely includes the calling to marriage and family life. For the common vocation of all Christians is fundamentally the same, to translate the love of God into the love of neighbor. In marriage, the nearest neighbor happens to be one's wife or husband!

VOCATION OF MARRIAGE

Vocations are always personal. They represent the way an individual person responds to his or her life unfolding before

God. As the two of you move toward marriage, you are preparing for a specific vocation. In a sense, you are in the midst of a vocational education course, but what you are preparing for is more than a job or career. It is your life together.

Because of the many ways in which marriage can be understood, it is important to be reminded of its God-given roots. In our secular society, it is easy for marriage to simply be thought about as "the next natural step." You've earned your education. You've gotten a job. You may be living away from your family of origin. You are "on your own." So what's next? It's time to get married. (In a similar way, when all your friends are getting married, you might feel pressure to do so, too.)

When you marry, however, you are invited to mature in a hurry. Your intellectual life, your emotional life and your social life can all move to new and deeper levels. That is, if you will let them. The personal adjustment of marriage brings one to the threshold of a new consciousness, a new awareness of life. It creates questions about life's real meaning, because your basic concerns are now not just your own. You both begin to explore what might be your shared visions and values. What changes confront you? How can you be faithful to each other? If you have different religious backgrounds, how will you work that out so your marriage is stronger? What are the two of you going to do about children?

Marriage forces a couple to realize that life is not made up of short-term or temporary arrangements. It's for keeps. Decisions must now be made in a broader context. Your love will be tested, the precise nature of your generosity exposed. Your baptismal commitment to make the reign of God more real will be brought to sharper focus in your new life together.

That is why marriage is a vocation.

LIGHT OF LOVE

When love is real, it allows the beloved to appear in the best possible light. This could be a problem in the sense that one may become blind to negative characteristics of the other which should be noticed. On the other hand, seeing goodness in another has the power of actually bringing forth a greater measure of goodness. Seeing the best calls forth the best. Such love tends to affirm, to enrich, and to assist the other's self esteem.

Many people grow up and live in a highly competitive environment where they are always trying to prove themselves. They never seem able to accept themselves "just as they are." Real love, however, works in the opposite way. It affirms the beloved right here and now. This acceptance allows the person to grow and develop in freedom, knowing that he or she is loved—warts and all.

Great marital love makes it much easier to bear the burden of daily life. True love pulls one's ego out of the center of the universe and puts it in context. By true love, one is freed, protected and constantly reaffirmed. This kind of love is quite different from possessive love, which is immature and destructive. The whole purpose of married love is to move the couple from "mine" to "ours."

Mature love also allows for the individuality of each marriage partner to be expressed. Marriage is not enforced togetherness, but, as the poet Rilke said, it is the protection of each other's solitude. Of course, what we are reflecting upon here is at the heart of the mystery of love. It is difficult to describe because it is the joining of a certain kind of togetherness with a certain kind of individuality, and these are not experienced as opposites. Rather, they exist in creative, life-enhancing tension which, when it happens between a wife and a husband, creates the best possible marriage.

RIGHT TO BE "OTHER"

Christian love reveals a right which can be easily over-looked. Part of keeping a marriage alive is each partner's willingness to allow, and even support, the right of the other person to develop his or her individual gifts. One of the greatest temptations in marriage is to want what is best for one's spouse—and to predefine what that might be! This insensitivity to the integrity of the other can surface when a serious argument arises. One spouse may expose his or her real feeling by exclaiming, "Oh, come on, be reasonable, do it my way!"

Without the light of love, married love can be turned into a tug of war. Partners can come to feel like two bodies joined at the hip. A false intimacy can confuse love with control. Unfortunately, couples are given little guidance in how to deal with everyone's right to be a unique individual. The answer to this danger in your relationship is not to imagine problems before they arrive, but to be sure that each of you understands and respects the other's individuality right from the beginning.

DAILY LOVING

Married love can sometimes be as fragile as a fine crystal wineglass. While the institution of marriage is quite resilient, it is a much better survival strategy for a couple not to be testing its limits. Rather, they should work at developing a nurturing attitude and lifestyle of "daily loving" right from the beginning.

The beauty and strength of the sacrament of matrimony as it is understood by the Catholic Church is that the individual spouses administer the sacrament to each other day after day. Their growth in intimacy and love becomes their special route to holiness.

The road is a winding one. Staying the course requires balancing shared interests with individual aspirations. The two of you should strive to maintain a workable balance between closeness and distance, between intimacy and separation, between dependency and independence. Through the sacrament of marriage, God promises the grace to meet this challenge as it rises before you.

POINTS FOR REFLECTION

1. There is a difference between "making a commitment" and becoming a committed person. Marriage is not only a mutual commitment "to do something" but a commitment "to be and become a new kind of person."

2. You can never fully understand another person because at the deepest level each person is a mystery. Yet the process of mutual personal revelation is part of what keeps marriage exciting and a never-ending story.

3. Marriage is not just the uniting of an "I" with a "You." It the creation of a new "We."

4. Your love for each other can be like God's love for each of us: an invitation waiting for a response, a call to the fullness of life together.

5. The source of marital happiness is established first within oneself.

QUESTIONS FOR DISCUSSION

1. Describe for each other marriages which you recognize as truly interdependent marriages. Also describe some which you consider either too dependent or too independent.

2. What do you think are the main reasons why marriages fail in the first few years? If you had to state what you think might be the "Achilles' heel" of your relationship, what would it be?

3. Look down the road a bit. How would you describe your marriage a year from now? What about five years ahead? Twenty-five years?

She stands at the altar and pledges her life . . . a life she just barely understands . . . pledges it "until death" to a man she also barely understands.

He takes her hand, places upon it a ring and speaks of his unending commitment to her, a woman as much a mystery to him as he is to himself.

And before their families, their friends, their community, and their God, they become one . . . forever.

But they are so young, and have much to learn about life, and love, and "forever."

And learn they will, to grow into that commitment . . . or out of it.

Barbara Ritter Garrison

LOOK OF LOVE

No word in the dictionary has more complicated and confusing meanings than the word "love." It's a good word; a great word; a powerful word. Yet it's also a dangerous word, full of mystery and excitement. Still, "love" is perhaps the best word we have available to describe your feelings and hopes for each other as you enter marriage. The more you understand love's complex meanings, however, the better you will be able to live in its light. And the more you live out the challenging demands of love, the more you will grasp its fullest depth and breadth.

WHAT IS LOVE?

No one has ever seen God.
Yet, if we love one another,
God remains in us,
and God's love is brought to perfection in us.
                                    1 John 4:12

Married love is a constant stretching forth of two people toward one another. It is a lifelong journey of the heart. Love demands a caring, supportive response from each partner. Love allows spouses to trust and believe that the beloved will never be knowingly hurtful or disrespectful.

Married love is generous giving, full sharing, benevolent thinking, consistent willing. It allows both parties to grow and mature into a relationship of wondrous beauty. In true love, each partner recognizes and fosters the individuality of the other. As the inner strength and convictions of the partners develop, they find it easier to take risks with each other.

ALONENESS

In his famous poem, "No Man Is an Island," John Donne reminded us with striking force of the human need for constant connections with other people. If we were left alone and isolated on an island, we might become terribly anxious, insecure, frightened and frustrated. We would have no one near us who could reflect back to us our personal goodness and assure us that we are desired, wanted and appreciated. We would be without someone to whom we could direct our time, attention, energy and goodness. We would have no one with whom we could share life's joys or sorrows. This would hurt, because each of us was created by the God of love with a huge desire to love and be loved. We all have a built-in craving for at least a small measure of recognition and acceptance from others.

On the other hand, a certain amount of loneliness is inherent to the human condition. Once we leave childhood and become aware of our ultimate dependence on ourselves and our own resources, and once we realize the sobering finality of our existence, even the most unreflective among us is bound to become aware of his or her ultimate aloneness. This basic aloneness, coupled with our equally basic need for others, is an inescapable dilemma of the human condition: each of us is autonomous; but none of us is totally self-sufficient.

Some people struggle against loneliness by losing themselves in the crowd. They seek a sense of belonging by adopting the appearance, the clothing, the habits and the lifestyle of a group. Others seek escape from being alone by becoming workaholics. Still others flee personal loneliness by entering superficial relationships with others, often falling into a series of meaningless encounters which may be intensified by the use of sex or drugs. These people cannot escape the trap of loneliness because they refuse to move to the level of deep intimacy.

RISK OF LOVE

Although the love found in marriage can relieve the pain of loneliness, the risk is often overwhelming. When you love, you give something of your inner self into the keeping of the other. You trust that the one who loves you will not harm you. Yet, if you allow each other to get close enough, you will know each other's weaknesses. You will know where the other is most vulnerable and best able to be hurt or even destroyed.

Most people today know of the sad and tragic stories of children who have been violated by parents or other caregivers. The tragedy of such events is that they happen to those who are supposed to be loved and cared for by those they trust completely. Defenseless and available, these children are harmed by those who are closest to them.

In marriage, couples face a similar situation. To love and be loved in its fullest measure, they are invited to be vulnerable, honest and open with each other. Wives and husbands joyfully choose to be their spouse's "most significant other." If the marriage then turns bad, it can be doubly painful—combining the pain of rejection with the pain of betrayal.

Serving as an expression of the mutual vulnerability of a married couple is the act of appearing before each other in physical nakedness. This is a rich, symbolic expression of unconditional availability. Unfortunately, in our society, this act has often become trivialized to the point of meaninglessness. It ends up being "no big deal."

Nevertheless, physical nakedness remains an important aspect of the psychological nakedness that forms the centerpiece of deep intimacy. Couples experience profound intimacy when each partner drops personal defenses and reveals his or her fears, hopes and weaknesses to the other. This is usually a gradual process. For example, Tom begins to learn of Susan's most vulnerable feelings, and Susan also becomes aware of Tom's greatest weaknesses. It is as if each was placing in the hand of the other a precious treasure. Each can do this because they trust the other to have the same care for the treasure as does its owner.

In moments of anger and argument, on the other hand, the sacred treasures can be smashed onto the hard floor of reality. With great care and deep vulnerability, Susan may once have revealed to Tom that one of her great fears was that she would become a complainer like her mother. Now, in the midst of an argument about Tom's being late for a date, he responds, "Now you're acting just like your mother. Complain, complain, complain."

Susan is terrified not so much by the argument as by

Tom's use of her secret fear, which she had told him in utmost confidence. Another old saying applies, "It really hurts to be hurt by a friend." Whenever partners reveal weaknesses and fears to each other, they should be labeled, "Fragile. Handle with Care."

Those who enter into the sacred space of intimate love enter a place where both wonderful and terrible things can happen. In their desire to find the great wonders, couples must risk experiencing the terror. They must risk the tragedy of a broken heart in order to gain the promise of a loving companion.

As you can see, we have traveled a far distance from that place where love is as simple as exchanging valentines or smiles across a crowded room. In the beginning of your marriage, love must be recognized as a demanding journey— one with many dangers and pitfalls, but with a glorious destination!

LOVE OF SELF

To be able to fully love another, it is critical that you first love yourself. While this may appear at first glance to be a contradiction, it is an important insight. Strong, lasting relationships require as "raw material" two strong individuals. Part of the beginning of a successful marriage is your personal conviction that you are worthwhile and lovable. The more secure you are in that conviction the more you will be capable of entering a deep, interpersonal relationship.

Those who enter marriage with feelings of personal insecurity and uncertainty are likely to try to use the relationship to make up for personal inadequacy. They will enter marriage more to take than to give.

Of course, you need not be reminded that relationships can be very complicated and confusing things. In the beginning of almost every relationship, you are more conscious of having your own needs fulfilled than of responding to the needs of another. But as time passes, true lovers begin to be concerned less for themselves and more for the beloved.

The best marriages are those which are based on this kind of other-centered love between two individuals who already love themselves. It may seem strange, but good marriages usually happen between women and men who really don't need to marry. They could go through life as single persons and be quite happy in doing so. But, instead, they freely chose the route of marriage.

Much of the popular language of romantic love, on the other hand, expresses "need love." How often have you heard song lyrics that have lines like, "I am nothing without you," or "I'll die if you ever leave me." Lines like those speak of an unhealthy dependence and an unrealistic expectation of love and marriage. If you think about it, these attitudes seem to say that marriage will "make up" for whatever one lacks. To use a helpful image, good marriages are not unions of clinging vines but of steadfast trees.

So that you don't become overly concerned, know that all people have their moments of insecurity and doubt. Many have days when they don't particularly like themselves. Most of us are not really satisfied with every aspect of our beings. The big question then is this: Do you love yourself enough so that you can truly connect and love another person?

INNER STRENGTH

One of the great weaknesses of our society is that it promotes pervasive competition without showing us at the same time how to be gracious and humble. We learn how to fight to win at an early age, but we often miss the lesson on how to be good winners and good losers.

How does this relate to marriage? Sometimes wife and husband can fall into patterns of competitiveness without even knowing it. An all too common theme on television and in movies is "the battle of the sexes." It also happens on tennis courts, in courtrooms, and in the boardrooms of our nation's corporations. And it can spill over into the living room and the bedroom.

Competitiveness in marriage can be fun in moderation, but it can wear down the more needed and important cooperative spirit. Remember, marriages survive because of the interior strength of the love between the wife and husband. We have just finished discussing the fragile vulnerability that is an important fact of intimate love. Both wife and husband usually know how to administer a "death blow" to their marriage. "Put downs" are terrible in any relationship; they can be almost fatal in a marriage. It is said that it takes more than twenty compliments to replace the damage done by one negative remark directed at one's spouse.

All this means that a relearning process may be in order if one is accustomed to using language more as a weapon than as a way to enrich others. The mocking banter that sometimes typifies contemporary dating rituals can wear thin inside a marriage. Instead of being competitive with their wife or husband, spouses need to show that they are on the other's side no matter what and to be attentive and generous in praise of each other. While positive expressions of affection and love may seem fairly natural in the first glow of marriage, it is most important to keep the light of marital love burning brightly. Familiarity can dampen enthusiasm. Routine can clog lines of communication.

Married love is founded on patience and a strategy suited for the long journey. Think of your marriage as a long-term investment in which every contribution made at any time contributes to the wealth. Usually it is the simple things which pay the biggest dividends. Not taking each other for granted, the exercise of simple courtesy, respect for each other's personal needs, a kind word when the other is having a bad day, a surprise gift—all these gestures, when taken together, will make your marriage worth all the money in the world.

RESPECT

I love you
Not only for what you are
But for what I am
When I am with you.
For putting your hand
Into my heaped-up heart
And passing over
All the foolish, weak things
That you cannot but help see there,
And for drawing out into the light
All the beautiful qualities
That no one else has ever looked
Quite far enough to see.

—anonymous

"Respect" comes from two Latin worlds—"re," which means "again," as in "return" or "remake," and "spicere," which means "to look" as in the word "spectator." Respect in marriage, therefore, means to look again, to notice what others do not, and to see in one's beloved qualities and characteristics only perceived by the eyes of true love.

You should first respect those qualities of your spouse which make him or her unique and special. This kind of perception begins with wonder, not with criticism. Unfortunately, many enter marriage with a secret plan to change or improve the other person. On the surface, this is explained as an act of love. After all, shouldn't you want to make the other person better than they are right now? Shouldn't you want what is best for your beloved?

The answer is "yes" and "no." The "yes" answer is that—if you are asked—you provide whatever assistance or support is asked for. The "no" answer comes from the fact that no one knows with certainty what's best for someone else. We may think or imagine we do, but we are easily deceived. Knowing what's best for the other can easily be confused with what we really want for ourselves.

A husband may say, for example, that he wants to help his wife become a better cook, but an outsider would pick up right away that the husband is really concerned for the state of his own stomach. Similarly, a wife may want to help her husband become more trim and have a better appearance, but what's really at play is her desire to "show off her catch" to admiring friends. Intentions can be very deceiving, and that is why marital love must always begin with respect for the uniqueness of one's spouse.

Take delight in the talents and accomplishments of your partner. Allow individual interests to blossom while at the same time trying to develop common interests and activities. The best graphic symbol for marriage is two circles which overlap partially, not totally. There is a kind of marriage called an "enmeshed" marriage in which couples are expected to do everything together. In fact, the goal of an enmeshed marriage is that both wife and husband think and feel exactly alike. This kind of marriage may be praised as "total oneness," but it is highly dangerous in real life.

Usually at the core of total togetherness is a single source of power. One decides, the other agrees. One leads, the other follows. It's like a cry and an echo—and the echo has no existence of its own. Often at the center of an enmeshed marriage, one will find what is basically a master/slave relationship.

Respect, on the other hand, creates the space needed for full individuality and full togetherness to exist within the same marriage. Love does not take away freedom but creates situations where both partners can be more free. Respect starts with that wonderful attitude of awe in which you silently look across the marriage bed and glimpse something of the mystery of that incredible someone with whom you have been blessed to share the rest of your life.

LOVE IS GIVING

While you are no doubt familiar with the phrase "it is better to give than to receive," this is not always an easy task. Nor is it better to give than to receive because it sounds more noble or generous. Giving is better than receiving because in giving we reach beyond the boundaries of the self and provide for the other person an enhanced and enriched understanding of his or her importance. We "build up" another person, and nothing is better than that.

The importance of the act of giving itself may not be obvious in the materialistic culture of our time. In television commercials, for example, people are usually shown as more excited upon the reception of something (the product) than in the providing of it.

Yet giving has a spiritual quality to it. When you give love to each other in marriage, you enhance the beloved's sense of dignity and personal worth. You reinforce the goodness and beauty of your partner. The best qualities of your spouse are drawn out. Couples who learn to share in love's abundance also learn something of the deep mystery of life itself, which is that each person's life is actually an expression of God's love.

LOVE IS THINKING, WILLING AND DOING

As humans who love, you will always be in a process of trying to learn what's best for your marriage. Another word for this process is "discernment." The word has a rich history in the Christian tradition. It means combining the best human ways of learning with a personal understanding of your life before God in order to make decisions best for you and your marriage.

In eight years of marriage, for example, Peter gave Martha a ranch house, a Jaguar, expensive jewelry and two international trips. He claimed that his love for her was the reason he spent long hours, even weekends, at his office. He wanted Martha to have everything she desired. Peter loved his wife according to his own idea of what he thought she wanted, and she seemed delighted to get all that "stuff." But he wasn't very *discerning* about her real needs.

Yet the foundation of genuine love is clear and honest thought, along with a will strong enough to make decisions which are truly best for the marriage. Martha needed more from Peter than things. She needed him to be there for her and to challenge her to find what she really wanted out of life. When they divorced, Martha had lots of possessions, but she was no better a person for having been married to Peter.

Emotional feelings in marriage are important, but love is more than warm sensations. Emotions can sometimes change like the weather. They can be affected by the performance of one's favorite athletic team. They can be determined by chemical changes within the body. Everyone has moods, good days and days we can't wait to end.

Love should be able to transcend these alterations of our emotional state. *Commitment* is the stabilizing force in a marriage. It is like the rudder of a sailboat. Despite the changes in the direction of the wind, it keeps a couple moving on a fixed course. Commitment unfolds through the joining of understanding with desire, the blending of thought and will. Commitment results in decisions which move one into action.

Philip's wife, Margaret, liked to take a drink (or two) after a hard day at the office. She claimed that it relaxed her. Over the first months of their marriage, her drinking routine was extended to include a few after dinner as well. Margaret began to fall asleep in the chair while watching the late evening news. Philip didn't say anything, because he sympathized with her pressure-packed job. He rationalized that everyone needs an escape from the problems of life. His approach was based on what he though love demanded—to support what his wife wanted. She wanted to drink and, because he loved her, he did not think he should deny this little pleasure.

Deep down, however, Philip knew that her life—and their marriage—was on a downhill slide. He knew that while his wife wanted alcohol, what she needed was help. He struggled with "interfering" in her life until he finally got enough courage and commitment to confront Margaret and insist that she get professional help.

True love requires strength of spirit. The Latin word for strength is "virtus," or "virtue." Virtue is love in action. Virtue, when faced with the difficulties of life, allows one to do difficult, loving things that are needed in a marriage—the things Philip did, and Peter did not.

THE OPPOSITE OF LOVE

Love is at once wondrous, joyful, fulfilling and challenging. People can be "swept off their feet" by love. Without constant nurturing and concern, however, love can be shattered on the hard rocks of reality. Some people used to think that a marriage could fly on automatic pilot. After Cupid's arrow struck its target, they thought little more needed to be done.

Now we recognize that this kind of thinking is totally naive. It is mistaken in the worst way, because it supports a myth which can destroy a marriage. The myth is partly based on the powerful emotional experience that love can be. Admittedly, the attraction of love can be overwhelming at times. But this "force" subsides, just as the calm comes after the storm. Romantic emotionalism can be a part of love, but it is more at the edge of love than at its center.

So, having reflected upon the heart of love, which is the commitment of one person to the good of another, we should turn our attention to love's opposite, which is not hatred but indifference. Hatred, while it is largely negative in spirit, still requires a connection with another. Indifference, on the other hand, implies separation.

It is sometimes said that most marriages end more with a whimper than with a bang. Loss of love is almost always a slow process of erosion. Its signs are boredom, taking each other for granted, and neglect. Couples falling out of love no longer take time to talk and do things together. The wife and husband occupy separate domains, each one living in a different world.

Due to the high divorce rate and based on the sober thought that not all marriages of indifference ever make it to the legal state of divorce, it is all the more necessary that successful marriages be viewed as a somewhat endangered species. They need a level of tender loving care that insures their survival in sometimes hostile or toxic circumstances.

No sane person enters marriage with the intent of eventual divorce. Even the most cynical spouse possesses hope for his or her particular marriage at the time of the wedding. Nevertheless, as the first days of wedded bliss turn into years of married life, the challenge of "keeping the home fires burning" becomes more real.

So be among those whose goal is to keep their marriage vital and virtuous. Keep growing as individuals and as a couple. Treasure your moments together and guard the sacred space you occupy as a couple. And know in your mind and in your heart that a marriage that is not daily being nourished and enriched is a marriage that is in some way slowly dying. Prepare yourself not just for the wedding but for the marriage.

POINTS FOR REFLECTION

1. While you may have been trained and educated to live in a competitive world, know that this pattern must be altered to succeed in the cooperative climate needed for marriage, where mutual trust, self-disclosure and love are the order of the day.

2. One of life's greatest challenges is to balance the healthy needs of the self with the needs of another. Good decisions in this area require open conversation, honesty and practical love.

3. Remember that no one stays on a high all the time. It is normal and natural to have good days and bad days, a condition which will affect both you and your marriage partner.

4. When you love another person, you undergo one of the deepest of all human transformations. Your world changes from a private one to a shared one as you open yourself to the love of another.

5. You would do well to decide each new day that you will make it a very important day in your marriage.

QUESTIONS FOR DISCUSSION

1. What things do you like to do alone? Which of them do you want to share with your marriage partner? What new areas of interest would you like to develop after you are married?

2. What do you consider your marriage partner's best traits? How do you intend to help him or her be "the best that he/she can be"?

3. What words or actions of your partner do you consider "put-downs"? What words or actions do you most like and feel build you up as a person?

"What is real?" asked the rabbit one day when they were lying side by side. "Does it mean having things that buzz inside you, and a stickout handle?" "Real isn't how you're made," said the skin-horse, "it's a thing that happens to you. When a child loves you for a long, long time—not just to play with—but really loves you, then you become real." "Does it hurt?" asked the rabbit. "Sometimes," said the skin-horse— for he always was truthful. "When you are real, you don't mind being hurt." "Does it happen all at once like being wound up, or bit by bit?" "It doesn't happen all at once. You become. It takes a long time. That's why it doesn't often happen to people who break easily, or have sharp edges, or have to be carefully kept. Generally, by the time you are real most of your hair has been loved off and your eyes drop out and you get loose at the joints and you're very shabby. But these things don't matter at all. Because once you are real, you can't be ugly, except to people who don't understand."

Margery Williams

Marriage is not . . .

commitment to an institution.

Marriage is . . .

commitment to a person,
a vision and a process.

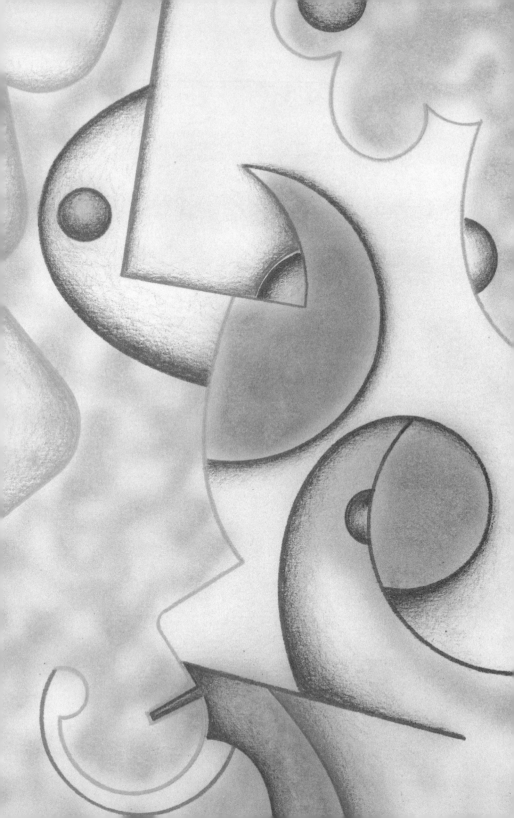

CREATIVE FIDELITY

The very ideas of loyalty, faithfulness, permanence are under attack today. We live in a world of rapid change, and we seem to be adapting so well that we now seem to prefer fast to slow. Our society offers us instant everything—from pudding to communication around the world through telephone, fax and modem. When we are forced to wait for anything, we grow anxious and irritated.

We have also become a nation of wayfarers. The average family now changes location every five years, and some move almost annually. Likewise, staying in the same job or career for one's adult lifetime is no longer considered normal or expected. Change is the order of the day. "New" is better than "old," "improved" beats "proven," "current" outshines "traditional."

With this kind of background, the notion of fidelity to one particular relationship may appear quaint and old-fashioned. We have learned to trade in and to replace that which is worn out. Why can't we apply this strategy to marriages as well?

THE TEACHING OF JESUS

For almost two thousand years, the words and actions of Jesus of Nazareth have influenced the direction people set in their lives. It is noteworthy that his insights and values seem to have weathered the test of time. His teachings, Christians hold, come from God.

On one fine day many years ago, Jesus stood in the presence of the lawyers of his day. These guardians of the Judaic law put a question to Jesus about one of the hotly debated issues of all times. They asked him where he stood on the issue of divorce. One school of thought, call them the conservatives, felt that divorce could only be granted for very serious reasons, such as adultery. Another school, more liberal in tenor, held that divorce could be granted for almost anything. (On their list of reasonable causes was that the wife was not a good cook!)

The assembled crowd grew silent as Jesus began to speak. "I do not believe in divorce, period," he said. "A husband must not leave his wife nor should a wife leave her husband. God wants marriage to last for a lifetime."

This was a position that was more stringent than even the most rigid view of the time. Everyone was taken back by his words. No doubt his own disciples received the news with open mouths. There is some indication in the Gospel that they later took Jesus aside just to make sure they heard him correctly.

But Jesus remained firm, despite their loud protests that his was a tough and demanding view. He assured them that they had heard right and that, yes, marriage was not intended as an easy arrangement. But, like all the commands of God, this one is a two-edged sword. While difficult to keep, it is also a path to great happiness. Jesus' message to us is that marriage is a glorious, extremely challenging, holy commitment.

CONTROLLING THE FUTURE

Part of the challenge of fidelity is that the road ahead is uncharted. People always change, so how can you know that you will want to remain married to a person after he or she changes?

When you think about it, however, marriage is no different from the many uncertainties which are part of life. No one can predict the state of their health a few days, much less years, ahead. Death of friends and family can come at any time. We are deceived if we attempt to live our lives as if everything is under our control. Very little falls in the category of the totally predictable.

When you enter marriage, it is quite appropriate to think about it as an adventure into the unknown. Surprises lay ahead which will make you quite excited and happy. The future also will offer you days of disappointment and sadness.

When you marry someone, you begin a walk into the wilderness. You promise that you will make this walk together. You agree in advance not to turn back or take separate paths. You realize that everyone makes mistakes, fouls up from time to time, and develops in ways that are surprising. Many marriage experts note that good marriages are usually seasoned with a sense of humor that allows couples to laugh at themselves. When Jesus said it is God's will that marriage be for a lifetime, he was not trying to come across as a spoilsport or to make life terribly difficult for others. Jesus was simply saying that fidelity is what is best for married couples. It may be what's needed to get them over some rough times. It allows them to always think in terms of the long journey ahead. Like good long-distance runners, couples need to "pace" their relationship. They need to keep the finish line in mind, not burn up all their energy right at the beginning.

Finally, Jesus understood that the unconditional acceptance necessary for a faithful marriage places a couple in a very special relationship to God. It is God's own nature to love without limit. When a couple attempts to express in their lives the same nature as God's, Jesus knew that God will give them the energy and grace they need.

PERMANENT AND EXCLUSIVE

The Christian ideal of marriage is that it be lifelong and exclusive. It is reasonable to ask the question, "Why?"

Some might simply say that this is a rule of the Church and that the case is closed. The law is clear and there are no exceptions. Couples should just grin and bear it. Life is supposed to be a challenge, and only the strong will survive.

But this teaching seems to be unreasonably harsh to many people. After all, God is the God of love and kindness, rich in mercy. Did God think up marriage on a bad day? Did God get up on the wrong side of the bed?

Step back some and reflect on the values which underly God's invitation to permanence. One of the most basic of all human needs is for security. Of course, this need can be carried to extremes when someone becomes unwilling to take any risks because there may be an uncertain outcome. Some risk, in fact, is essential in life if we are to continue to grow.

The kind of normal security humans seek, however, is

more like an environment in which others can be counted on to provide at least some assurance and protection. It's like the rules of a football game. Given the inherent violence of the game, the rules provide a structure that allows people to play without getting hurt. Reasonable security allows one to be free and playful. Security is not intended to be restrictive but to be directive. It focuses one on what's important.

One of the most important outcomes of permanence in marriage is the development of trust. A relationship of trust does not just kick in full blown on the wedding day. It builds gradually through countless experiences in which each partner gives to the other proof of dependability and reliability. Each one learns to rely on the other. Each one begins to take comfort in the belief that his or her spouse will be there through thick and thin—until "death do them part."

Another outcome of permanence is that a married couple can relax in the joy of their relationship. They don't have to feel that they are always being put to the test or on trial. Their love does not have to be proved over and over again in the face of an anxious future.

You can easily imagine the quality of a marriage where each spouse is constantly worried that the other one might leave and not return. In fact, given the generally precarious state of marriage, it is of no surprise that a ton of stress and nervousness occurs in many marriages over just this issue.

If a couple really accepts that marriage means that they are "together forever," they will not see every problem, every disagreement, as a potential disaster. They will not be asking themselves day after day, "Is this it? Is this the breaking point?" They will be able to take the ups and downs of marriage in stride and deal with difficulties as they come. Belief in marital permanence does not exempt a couple from the challenges of dealing with differences or of resolving conflicts. But it does create a climate where judgments can be made against the big picture of a long life together. Further, the fact that they are committed for life also seems to strengthen a couple's desire to deal with difficulties before problems escalate beyond control.

In Christian marriage, there is also the challenge of exclusiveness. In some traditional wedding vows, we find the phrase "while forsaking all others." The "giving up" of others need not be viewed as a negative demand. Rather, it implies that one's primary energy, one's basic focus, will remain exclusively on one's wife or husband.

This does not mean that married people cannot have friends of the opposite sex. In fact, friendship with others of both genders is part of the healthy and wholesome Christian life. Marital love, however, is a very special, focused love. It is a deeply intimate love. This means that the central place of love in one's life is, so to speak, already taken. It also means that when one is attracted to others, one will treat the attraction as perhaps interesting, but not serious. Self-discipline in this context is not only a virtue but a survival skill. The totality of the marital commitment is so profound that there is no room for others in the marriage bed.

PROMISES

Real promises have the power to direct one's life toward treasures unimaginable. Marriage vows possess even greater force because they are made not only between two free, aware and loving persons but also expressed publicly in the presence of each partner's family, friends and fellow church members. They are made to each other, to others, and to God—all at the same time.

Marriage contains a wonderful paradox. While the couple should never take each other for granted, they do! This means that, while they must frequently nurture their mutual love with consideration, attention and imagination, they can also relax in the knowledge that their love is real and strong. They do not start from square one each morning. They know that their relationship can handle the stress and storms of daily life. Each one has a rich reserve from which to draw energy and hope. Above all, each knows that the other wants the marriage to work and will do what has to be done to make that happen.

If Ted remembers, for example, that he was a real jerk the day before and wonders whether Carol might leave him for good, he certainly will not get done much work that day. If Mark is really late one night and Sue worries that he may be out with another woman, she will be overwhelmed with anxiety.

If marriage were a matter of constant testing, doubting, or trying to win the favor of one's spouse, couples would never mature either individually or together. Just like a house, a marriage needs a good foundation. The marriage vows of fidelity, permanence and exclusivity provide the best environment for love to develop and for children to be reared.

That is why the Church teaches that there is no such thing as a healthy "trial marriage." As soon as the conditions of "as long as it works out" or "as long as we are both really happy" are added to the relationship, something essential disappears.

It is called *commitment.*

VITALITY

Fidelity in marriage is not merely a matter of "staying together" as an end in itself. It is interesting to note, however, some of the common patterns which provide such "stability" to certain marriages.

Some couples live in what is called a *conflict-habituated* marriage. It is almost as if the wife and husband need each other because they enjoy fighting. "A day without a good argument is hardly worth getting out of bed for" would be their philosophy. They feed on various forms of attacking, hurting and conquering each other. Tension fills their days and nights. While they may be responding to a need in each other, it would be difficult to justify this kind of life as worthy of any healthy person.

Others stay together in what might be called a *devitalized* marriage. Opting for peaceful coexistence at all costs, they live quiet, respectful, boring lives. They are passive observers to what's happening around them, mostly because virtually nothing is happening between them! Their marriage is an emotional wasteland, but they remain married partly because the thought of doing anything else seems like too much trouble. Sadly, they may justify their marriage with a kind of perverted, self-righteous religious argument.

In stark contrast to these types of "stable" marriages is the marriage of *vitality*, which is characterized by a sharing of life's many great and sad moments. Between the wife and husband in a vital marriage is a many-stranded psychological bond which nourishes growth in both. They live within their commitment to a lifelong relationship. Their love is focused and faithful. Their sexual intercourse symbolizes the unconditional availability of each to the other. Their marriage is a constant learning experience. They are always searching for better ways to communicate, to deal with the inevitable conflicts which come between two different people. And because life is never perfect, they have also developed patterns of forgiveness and laughter which remind them that the goal of perfection is always only on the horizon.

All the messy and surprising moments of life are shared by such couples. They demonstrate a willingness to share not only strengths but also weaknesses. They share privacy, bed, nakedness, sickness, hopes, fears, secrets, family ties, pregnancy, old age and even death. Enriched by their fidelity to each other, they can walk life's long journey hand-in-hand, knowing that they have lived in the presence of human goodness.

FOREVER, BUT HOW?

A lifelong, vital marriage is a great work of art. Its composition gradually gains definition and beauty each day. Trust, mutual appreciation and deep love develop gradually but unceasingly, much like the movement of a glacier toward the sea. The couple's sense of "we-ness" or the notion of "two in one flesh" found in the book of Genesis, is integral to their marriage.

You will note that marriage is being presented here more as a process than a state of life. This is a very important insight into the experience of marriage. In this view, marriage is considered as much a task to be accomplished as it is some club of which one is a member. One of the most important realizations a couple must come to is that marriage must be "worked on" day after day and that its continuance as a vital relationship depends on daily attention and nurturing.

By sharing their daily lives, a couple continuously creates

their marriage. It takes on a meaning to them that is really not available to the scrutiny or judgment of outsiders. The couple's level of mutuality and interdependency is known to them, but others will never see it in its full richness. The couple become "existentially indissoluble"—that is, they grow together in a way that, even given the chance to separate easily, they will choose not to. They know instinctively that remaining married to each other is the best and most satisfying way they can live their lives.

Couples like this are not just lucky. They work hard and play hard at their marriages. They enter marriage sure of their decision, but are also aware that they are amateurs who have much to learn. They know that they will need to continually energize their relationship in the days and years ahead. For them, the phrase "settling down" is unrealistic and stupid. The wedding signifies a beginning, not an end.

What keeps them together is their love, which is an active—not a passive—force in their lives. They make adjustments and work out their differences. They respect each other's individuality, carry one another's burden, and think not only about the lifetime task of daily marriage but about the daily tasks of lifelong marriage.

INFIDELITY AND FAITHFULNESS

It is because the marital vows are so sacred and the trust between couples must be so complete that infidelity to one's marriage partner is so devastating. The most obvious, and in many ways the worst, form of infidelity is adultery—sex with someone else outside the marriage. The discovery of this betrayal, no matter what the reason, no matter how sincere the apology, destroys the sense of exclusivity upon which the intimacy of the married couple is built.

The mass media—books, tabloids, television and the movies—often make light of adultery. Often, the phony argument that an affair adds "spice" to a marriage is offered as justification. Don't believe it. Ask who is making this assertion. Is it someone who is happily married? Never! The mockery made of marriage by Hollywood is pervasive. Nevertheless, people can be confused by a clever artistic portrayal of an affair that seemingly adds to the quality of a marriage, without any negative consequences or repercussions. What is put in a movie as fiction in this case remains pure fiction. In truth, it is unconnected in any way with real life.

Beside a sexual "affair," however, one can also speak about non-sexual infidelity. It is possible to develop an inappropriate intimate relationship with another person without ever crossing the line of having sexual intercourse. If, for example, one spouse turns to another person—a friend or a coworker perhaps—for the sharing and support he or she should be seeking from the other spouse, it could be a form of unfaithfulness.

Likewise, you can allow things—a job, a hobby, the television set—to get in the way of fidelity to your spouse. Any time anything or anyone takes the place of the primacy one's spouse should hold, it smacks of infidelity. Your wife or husband should never feel that she or he must settle for second place.

Still, marital fidelity need not be viewed as a ball and chain. While some think that the obligation of fidelity is merely the Church's way of keeping people in line, it actually contains many positive features which deserve our attention. Fidelity in marriage is good for the marriage and good for the married.

It builds trust between spouses and character in each of them. Fidelity flows from the marriage promises and allows them to be kept.

Just as it is said that good wine takes time to mature, much the same can be said of marriage. Almost everything that is important to a person—the search for truth, the gaining of skills, the quest for deep happiness—require a process of unfolding. In our heart of hearts, we all know this. So how, then, does the following proposal sound? "Darling, I love you. The sun rises and falls on your beauty. I need you and I want you beside me. I cannot live without you. Will you marry me for a year and a half?"

CHILDREN

Up to now, we have limited our discussion of marriage to the relationship between the two spouses. This was done because that relationship is the foundation for all family life. While you no doubt know many single parents, even they will most likely affirm that it's best that children be raised by two parents, a mom and a dad, if at all possible.

Therefore, it seems appropriate to mention here the value of fidelity between a couple to any children who come into the marriage by either birth or adoption. With so much pressure on family life today, it seems all the more important to underscore the value of permanence in the marital relationship to children. There is simply no exact replacement for a loving set of parents who stick together through thick or thin. And, most likely, there never will be.

TAKE ME ALONG

In the midst of our call for permanence and stability in marriage, we should also mention how change is a part of any realistic portrait of life. "Change" may be one of the most important words of our era. It is said that we have witnessed more change in world events, in science and technology, in product development and entertainment, and in whatever other category you might like to list than any previous generation in human history.

We have to add to that list the obvious fact that people also change. Lifecycle studies are everywhere. The span of human life is being divided up more and more each day. A century ago life was simply divided into childhood and adulthood. Around fifty years ago, a new category of people came into this picture. They were named adolescents. Even more recently, we have had described for us various other ages and stages of life. Each of these stages is marked or caused by changes—physical, psychological, mental, spiritual. From all of this, we can conclude a simple axiom: To be human is to change.

How does this relate to marriage? Think of it this way: Marital love is like loving a moving target. Over the years, you and your partner will change and develop new interests and values, your energy level will alter, you will develop new awareness of yourself and of each other. Marriage is a living, dynamic relationship. If it is rooted in a deep, healthy friendship between the two of you, you will not only tolerate these changes, you will celebrate them.

Realize that the rate of change may vary from person to person. Oftentimes, people change quickly—even dramatically—when they experience a formal education or start a new career. The arrival of children also brings dramatic change.

One partner may delight in being a parent, while the other may take some time to get used to the idea.

Differing rates of change between a couple need not be a problem if the situation is acceptable to both the wife and husband. Where there is mutual respect, each partner allows the other adequate space for individual personal development. It is difficult to discuss this need in the abstract, because each marriage is different in terms of what might be called healthy togetherness and healthy autonomy. This is, however, a major matter for discussion within a marriage. Just keep in mind, there are three components needing attention: you, your partner and your marriage. Balancing the needs of all three is an important facet of the art of marriage.

Every person enters marriage with a bag full of personal interests and favorite things to do. Couples preparing for marriage go through a natural process of determining what's in each one's bag, and they are delighted in the discovery of common items: "It's wonderful, we both like new wave jazz, sky-diving, and anchovy thick crust pizza. We're a match!" Often the decision to marry will be explained to outsiders based on these kinds of common interests.

All couples, however, sooner or later also discover that each partner has many interests that the other does not share. This is fine, too. There's nothing wrong with married people pursuing separate activities. "Absence makes the heart grow fonder," and all that.

Still, it is usually a good idea to invite your spouse to join you in your special passions, and it is an equally good idea to show a willingness to try (or at least to tolerate) your mate's hobbies and interests. "Take me along," and "Would you like to come with me?" are two excellent phrases for married couples to learn . . . and to use often.

Another good strategy is to develop new common interests after the wedding. These new activities would be a product of your marriage and equally shared. It is a good indicator of unselfish love to show a willingness to learn to enjoy life with and through the other person. Nevertheless, remember that forcing participation or interest on an unwilling spouse does not benefit a marriage. You're not going to change a rock-and-roll fan into a classical music enthusiast overnight—if ever!

Neither is it possible for spouses to be the sole source of stimulation for each other. You both need outside people with whom you can share certain aspects of your lives, people who have common interests, people you can depend upon for help and understanding.

If all this sounds complicated, it is! But it's also worth figuring out, just as Connie has.

CONNIE'S STORY

My name is Connie. I'm 55 years old. I've had this face a long time, and I've earned every crease in it. I have a husband, three children, and five grandchildren.

Mac and I have lived a great deal in 30 years. We're together, and we're the best of friends. What about tomorrow? Ask me tomorrow. We've survived lost jobs, Vietnam, a daughter in the front bedroom for two years with rheumatic heart disease, and a teen-age son who got into drugs rather heavily. We've prevailed against a sexy widow who had Mac all staked out and against a handsome, lonely neighbor who said he needed me very much.

I'm supposed to tell you about "creative fidelity." Fidelity has been the key to our life together. Being married is never once-and-for-all; it's a challenge every morning, every season.

Most people think infidelity means climbing into bed with somebody. That's the least of it. Sam Green, our neighbor, has been unfaithful to his wife, Lucy, through ledgers, bank statements and sales charts. That first concern—that center of attention a wife needs—he gave to his business; Lucy got what was left. Carol Williams, who lives down the street, is what I call "a married mother." She's unfaithful to her husband because her children get her attention first and her constant care. If one of them develops a hangnail, it's a crisis. Bill Williams is just part of the furniture.

I've seen men unfaithful to their wives through their mothers, fishing and cars, and I've seen women unfaithful to their husbands through their jobs, housekeeping and even church work. If this "infidelity" lasts long enough, the neglected partner may well take off as soon as somebody shows some real human interest in him or her, or else the couple may spend dull years just tolerating each other. Creative fidelity, on the other hand, means taking the time to be continually sensitive to the other's needs. It means using imagination to stimulate and interest the partner.

Creative fidelity includes supporting the partner when he or she wants to do something. Like the time Mac wanted to take a couple of courses at the local junior college. Two days later, I was saying, "Here are some brochures from the college for you. Most of the good things are on Mondays and Thursdays. I'll switch my bowling night to Wednesdays and come over and audit one of those Thursday classes with you." That's a lot different from saying, "OK, go if you want to."

Creative fidelity can also be confronting. Like the time I got upset at the young couple next door. She had been on the block for only about two months and had already become extremely popular. I began making unkind remarks about her, until Mac came in one night and—in his kind and easy way—said, "Listen, friend, I'm a little troubled about some of the things you've been saying about the Bryans. Maybe we are not being quite fair to them. Let's invite them over a couple of times and get to know them better."

When Mac wanted to risk our savings to start a new business, I was very nervous. But I knew he had to give it a try, so I supported him—scared to death inside, but as energetic and enthusiastic as I could be. Between you and me, I think I supplied the support he needed to make the whole thing work.

POINTS FOR REFLECTION

1. The intensity of experiences and feelings in early marriage may be no index of its permanence.

2. Although marital infidelity is always wrong, the offended spouse may not always be "innocent."

3. Infidelity may result from the gradual, unrecognized and unadmitted process of becoming deeply, emotionally involved with a third party. Be careful not to undervalue the positive side of jealousy. It may be a warning sign that something is not right.

4. Nobody is perfect. The danger of thinking your spouse was "made for you" is that you may be denying reality, which may inhibit healthy marital adjustment.

5. To be faithful may involve some challenge to one's spouse. It is all right to ask for help or favors from your wife or husband.

QUESTIONS FOR DISCUSSION

1. Share stories about fidelity and infidelity in other people's marriages, and try to name what went wrong or what went right . . . and why.

2. How do you feel about your spouse having good friends of the opposite sex? What do you consider to be the ideal way for both of you to handle friends outside your marriage?

3. In your personal view, why is fidelity so important in many aspects of life? Why is it absolutely critical in marriage?

How do I love thee?
        Let me count the ways.
I love thee to the depth
        and breadth and height
My soul can reach,
        when feeling out of sight
For the ends of Being
        and ideal Grace.
I love thee
        to the level of everyday's
Most quiet need,
        by sun and candle-light.
I love thee freely,
        as men strive for Right;
I love thee purely,
        as they turn from Praise.
I love thee
        with the passion put to use
In my old griefs,
        and with my childhood's faith.
I love thee
        with a love I seemed to lose
With my lost saints—
        I love thee with the breath,
Smiles, tears, of all my life!
        —and, if God choose,
I shall but love thee better
        after death.

Elizabeth Barrett Browning

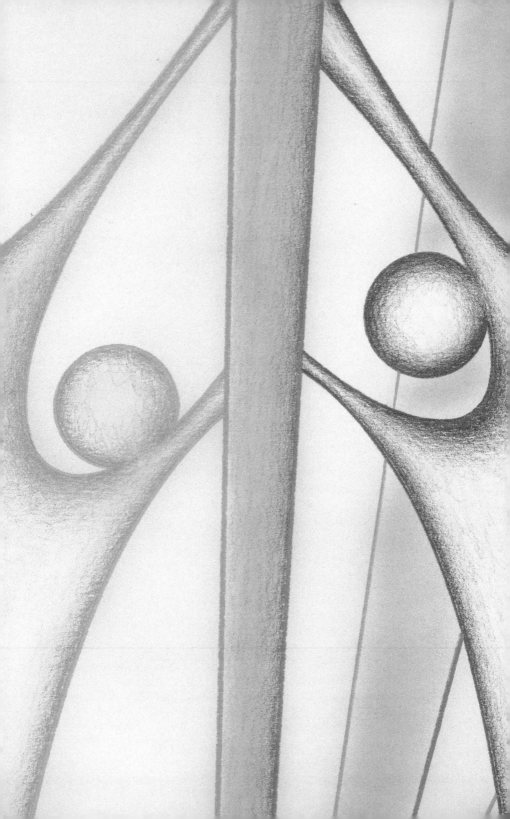

BUILDING RELATIONSHIP

Building a strong, caring, faithful marital relationship is a slow, deliberate yet exciting process that may be likened to two porcupines approaching each other for warmth. If they stay too far apart, they remain cold. If they come too close together, they can hurt one another. In marriage, establishing just the right distance for honest and healthy intimacy takes good communication and caring. It is also something that usually needs to be learned.

DIFFERENT IN MANY WAYS

Everyone tends to interpret what's going on in a relationship in terms learned from his or her past history of training and experience. As one pioneering psychologist put it, "We all peep out at the world through our own separate knotholes. We see everything through the unique lens of our own mindset."

You have been conditioned by years of experience with people close to you. So has the person you are marrying. Never are these experiences exactly alike. Some people's experiences have prepared them wonderfully for marriage. Others have been affected in a very negative way. For most, it has been a mixed bag.

For example, each of your families established rather precise ways of dealing with problems and disagreements. Likewise, each had its own ways of expressing affection and warmth. Some of these were good, some bad. But they are all learned behavior that will carry over into your marriage.

It is a serious mistake to assume that just because you love another person he or she will react to situations the same way you do. You have heard the phrase, "opposites attract," and this is true in many, many marriages. Certainly you two have many similarities, but part of why you are attracted to each other is based on your differences. Perhaps you recognize in your partner other qualities which you wish you possessed. Maybe you know of something in yourself which you judge the other could use. You may be neat and tidy. The other may be a slob. He or she may be outgoing and a social animal. You may be overly quiet and reserved. The point is that you are almost surely *different* in many ways.

INFLUENCE OF FAMILY OF ORIGIN

In modern society, we are brought together in many ways to become more alike. We can label these processes "equalizers." People from different families watch the same television shows, see the same movies, and go to the same schools. Nevertheless, each family retains its own way of appreciating or interpreting these "shared" experiences.

More and more, we are learning of the important role played by our "families of origin"—the families in which we were raised. What's most interesting and some say even mysterious about the family of origin phenomenon is how a family's power of influence extends back for many generations. We are, in a sense, where we came from—and *from whom* we came. Many historians of culture note that family-based learning starts very early in life when we are taught the relative importance of family, marriage, and family connections. For some families, these social relationships are extremely important. Others families tend to promote very loose family ties.

Deeply ingrained family practices, customs, loyalties, biases, class distinctions, ethnic prejudices, sexual attitudes, and so forth are slow to change. The effect of family and ethnic background on a marriage is deeper and more pervasive than most people recognize. Even as you create your own new family, you are in a very real way marrying each other's family.

One of the positive benefits of a marriage where each spouse comes from a different family background is that each can enrich the other with what's best in his or her tradition. Furthermore, their children have the benefits of more than one tradition to draw from. It is important for couples to avoid a judgmental attitude on the other's different ways, although this is often more easily said than done. More typical is the human response of defensiveness when faced with such differences.

The key thing for a married couple to keep in mind—always—is that difference does not necessarily imply better or worse, right or wrong. Different simply means not the same.

INFLUENCE OF COURTSHIP

In the process of dating, you discovered and responded to many attractive qualities in each other—his liveliness, the way she laughs or can put people at ease, her seriousness or his relaxed nature. You learned about many interests you held in common. You like the same kind of music. You are bothered about the same social issues. As time passed, you informally compared your personalities, likes and dislikes, goals and values, and found that you fit together fairly well. This kind of judgment is particularly important when you move from the dating game to the more serious process of court-ship. Finally, you decided that you loved each other well enough to take a deep breath and say, "Let's get married."

During an engagement period, however, most couples are on their best behavior. You already know that the other person likes you. You can guess the specific personal qualities in you which attract his or her interest. You then "feature" those qualities as much as you can, because you want the relationship to deepen each day. You are also on guard to prevent anything that might destroy the relationship.

Such behavior obviously has its value, but it can also be dangerous. In the courtship period, you both have a "vested interest" in maintaining the relationship. You both, presumably, want to get married. Your betrothed is the best prospect you've had in a long time—or perhaps ever will have. Neither of you want to blow it.

This attitude, however, can play tricks on your percep-tions. It's like looking at your beloved through a pair of binoculars. When you see desirable qualities, you use the end that magnifies the object in view. When you see the traits you consider negative, you turn the binoculars around and, presto, the problems don't seem very large or important. You might even have a tendency to say, "Oh, he'll give that up after we're married," or "She isn't really like that." You've heard it before, but take It seriously now: "Love is blind."

LIVING TOGETHER

Many couples today try "living together" before marriage. For some, it's merely the most convenient way of having sex before marriage. They simply can't wait, even though they know that what they are doing is wrong. Others rationalize that living together is a valid way of learning more about the person they intend to marry. It's like having a "free home trial" of a product before you actually buy it.

The question which must be faced, however, is this: Does living together or "cohabitation" before marriage really provide better information about your compatibility than if you continue living apart in the traditional manner? The answer is clear from research concerning this important issue.

This research shows, basically, that those couples who live together before the wedding are blinded by the same processes that exist for those who live separately. In fact, the danger of perceiving the other in the best possible light is magnified by cohabitation. The reason for this seems to be that living together as a test of compatibility is strongly influenced by the insecure nature of the arrangement. Since a couple is not married, the uncertainty of their relationship is often overcompensated. They often attempt to make their relationship seem more secure by either ignoring weaknesses or focusing only on the strengths.

In other words, couples who live together before marriage are even more challenged to be on their best behavior than those who don't. What's worse is that any dysfunctional patterns of relating which they develop while living together are not easily discarded once the couple is, in fact, married. It is no wonder, then, that statistics definitely show that those who live together before marriage have no better chance at marital success than those who don't. Further, studies also show that couples who live together before marriage are more likely to engage in extramarital affairs during their marriages. This may be a further indicator of the lack of a developed maturity on the part of such spouses.

Finally, we cannot overlook the situation where the invitation "to move in with me" is nothing more than an invitation to be used by the other person. Selfishness, or the more current phrase "self-absorption," may be at work here. Misuse of another person was not invented in this century, you know. Because of the widespread practice of cohabitation before marriage in our society, however, things have reached a point where social pressure has become a major force. Traditional ways have been labeled "old-fashioned" or even "destructive." Nevertheless, now that we have had some long-term experience of extensive cohabitation and have studied its effect, it is time to call for a reversal of this practice and describe it for what it is—a poor preparation for marriage!

PROCESS OF MARITAL ADJUSTMENT

"Adjustment" is not a bad word in marriage. It does not indicate weakness or loss of personal integrity. Rather, it points to the normal, healthy process of moving from the single life to a life of intimate sharing with another. Adjustment begins with listening and observation. It also includes expressing honestly and clearly one's personal needs and desires in the relationship. Finally, it means stating what's bothering you, what confuses you, or what you are having difficulty in understanding.

Adjustment in marriage indicates personal growth and movement toward the other person. It is a special way of expressing one's love and interest in one's spouse. In good marriages, the adjustment process occurs in both the wife and the husband. The movement is balanced and more or less equal. If it is one-sided, it means that one spouse is giving in and the other isn't. The one who gives in all the time, however, may be playing the role of martyr, which is unhealthy and will eventually haunt the marriage.

Adjustment is not submission. If one partner is afraid to express needs or make requests, or desires peace at any price, a relationship quickly becomes sour. In the other extreme, both partners "dig in" and resist making any adjustments whatsoever. What follows is a gradual growing apart, the development of separate lives, and the disintegration of the marriage.

Adjustment can be a wonderful expression of love. It calls forth creativity and imagination. To use the image of building construction, adjustment is like the engineering process of combining two types of structural systems (in this case one female and one male). Each has special properties which, when united, make the final structure stronger and more beautiful. But the two systems must be carefully aligned to fit each other for maximum strength and endurance. The good news is that this process of alignment in marriage has been happening with a fairly high success rate throughout history. The bad news is that as long as the building stands, some ongoing adjustment is necessary to keep it upright.

DECISION-MAKING

Every day, all of us are confronted with decisions. In a way, we are very fortunate, because a few short centuries back, ordinary people had precious few decisions to make. In fact, the norm was that even marriages were arranged for them so that they did not even have to make that decision.

Every decision is made up of two parts: the process of reaching the decision and the actual decision itself. In marriage, the process is a hundred times more important than the decision.

Ideally, all decisions affecting the marriage should be joint ones. When both the wife and husband participate in equal measure in the process, both have ownership of the result. Many businesses are discovering that participatory management can be an important way of creating better organizations. In marriage, the same is true, only more so.

To be sure, in making important decisions, clear disagreement can and often should arise between a wife and husband. It could be a question of where to live, when to try to have children, or whether it is time to make a major purchase.

In these cases, each partner must speak his or her views. Although sometimes very difficult, it is beneficial for one or the other to take a bit of a leap in the direction of a solution. For instance, you might say, "Well, it doesn't look like we're going to agree on this and, since I got my way last week, let's go your way this time." If, after reasonable discussion, a couple is close to agreement but not quite there (this is normal and happens regularly in most marriages), then it is helpful to ask who has more stake in the decision and which result will most positively impact the marriage. Or, if possible, it may be a good thing to just postpone the decision until circumstances change.

We earlier introduced the concept of discernment. The process of discernment, where one looks at what's going on from all possible angles—including values and religious beliefs, can be used in this context. Remember, the object of decision-making is not to win or lose but to make the best decision for *both* of you. Every time there is a clear winner and a clear loser in your decision-making, the loser may become bitter and disturbed. Many marriages are made or destroyed around this issue of decision-making, so be sure to devote good time and energy in this matter.

You are now a team, so once a play (a decision) has been called, devote your full, combined effort to make it work. Couples in trouble often have created subtle systems of sabotaging themselves. For example, while it's often tempting to declare after something has failed, "I told you so," these four little words have a way of etching a wound into the defeated person that is not easily healed or forgotten.

AN EXAMPLE OF COMPROMISE

Let's examine the adjustment process from another angle and see how it might look as a mythical couple, Fred and Sarah, tries to work out a common challenge in early marriage—namely "the in-laws!"

1. They consider many of the issues at stake in the situation.

   * "Our relatives would like us to visit them as often as we can."

   * "We want to remain in contact with them, but, although we have a generally good relationship with all of them, we also know of some 'hot spots.' "

* "We don't want to get trapped in a pattern where we will be expected to visit more than we want and have that pattern go on for years!"

2. They individually consult their feelings about these issues.

   * "I really don't mind visiting our relatives. The food is good, but after a couple of hours I get bored."

   * "His father is fine, but he likes to start debates and I get angry."

   * "I get anxious when her mother wants to know every little detail about our life."

   * "I know that our parents have given us a lot and I would feel guilty if we just avoided them. I feel obliged."

3. They share their feelings with each other.

   * "We both respect our parents. We know they are hoping for grandchildren and our staying in touch is very important to them."

   * "We're not sure our parents really know deep down that we have left the nest. They seem to want to interfere in areas that are our private concern."

4. They determine what is most at stake in their decision.

   * "Sarah, you are the only child of a very possessive mother and father."

   * "Fred, you are one of six children. Most of them are living somewhere else."

5. They discuss the effect of their decision and who will suffer major consequences.

   * "If we don't visit your folks regularly, Sarah, we'll never hear the end of it."

   * "If we don't visit your parents, Fred, especially when many of your sisters and brothers are in town, we will eventually lose touch with your whole family."

6. They find out how their married friends and other people they know solve similar problems.

   * "Your sister cannot get home very often because of lack of money right now, but she calls every weekend."

   * "My parents used to spend Christmas eve with one set of their parents and Christmas day with the other."

7. Having considered and discussed all these factors, they try to agree on some guiding principles for their marriage.

   * "We'll try to keep the schedule of our visits flexible and not fall into a fixed pattern."

   * "We'll try to do things with our relatives, rather than just sit around and talk."

   * "We'll see them more often than we would chose but less often than they would like."

   * "We'll make no major commitments in this area without first clearing it with each other."

PERSONAL HABITS

What usually makes or breaks a marriage are not the big things, but the scores of little benefits and annoyances. Here are some of the common areas of potential tension:

* Appearance. Will his underwear-and-bare-foot approach offend her? Will her wearing curlers on weekends bother him? Will he be expected to shave every day? Can one buy clothes without approval from the other?

* Privacy. Does she need quiet time alone to sort out all the many parts of her life? Can he invite his friends into all parts of the house? How do both feel about bathroom privacy? Do either get disturbed when the other listens in on phone calls?

* Social Life. What if she wants one night out a week with her girl friends? Do they want to go grocery shopping together? What about his old girl friends? How much time do they devote to developing social ties with people from work?

* Entertainment. How much football watching is too much? How often do they want to see movies at the theater? What about cultural events? She likes hard rock and he enjoys classical music. Do they each endure the other's taste, go their separate ways, or find a type of music they both can enjoy?

* Housekeeping. How clean is clean? What's the difference between casual and sloppy? What standards are they both comfortable with? Who does what in terms of cleaning?

* Rhythm of the Day. Is he a morning person and she a night person? What patterns best suit each one for eating, exercise, leisure?

* Ritual. When is early and when is late? How much preparation time is needed before guests arrive? Is there a regular time for prayer or is it best left spontaneous? What kind of sexual activity do they each enjoy? What rituals or customs do they bring from their families of origin?

GENDER ROLES

The traditional roles of wife and husband have changed dramatically over the last few years. With so many women now working outside the home, new schedules, new expectations and new agreements seem appropriate. Most marriages today value the full equality of wife and husband. They express this by sharing all the tasks associated with housekeeping, finances, social life, etc. In the past, the wife's role was often bound to the home. She "ruled" in domestic matters. He "ruled" outside the home. This so-called division of labor was fairly fixed.

Now, just about everything seems up for negotiation. Each marriage must develop its own role patterns, and this is how it should be. There is no one ideal blueprint for determining what's best. Here is where marital creativity is so important. Many will allow circumstances to play an important role. For example, when both work at different places, and one is delayed because of a late meeting, the other begins to prepare their supper. On the other hand, it is important to have some of these kinds of things worked out ahead of time. This prevents misunderstanding and hurt feelings. When too much is "up for grabs," it's best to get things "tied down" whenever possible.

Also be aware of the gender role expectations that each person brings into a marriage. We all learn so much of this from our parents. It's so deep that many people are simply unaware of its influence. Often, we assume that whatever the expectation—e.g., men take out the garbage, women clean bathrooms—everyone accepts the pattern and it is written in stone. All of this merits discussion. Your dealing with these matters early in your marriage will be of great help. In some ways, the patterns of marriage are like newly poured cement. When the cement is fresh, you can move it around and shape it into almost any form. But wait too long and further change is all but impossible.

EMPLOYMENT PATTERNS

There are many nuances to the theme, "marriage and work." Married women often react with righteous hostility when asked, "Do you work?" While the questioner may really be asking whether the woman has a job outside the home, there still remains the implication that unless she's bringing home a paycheck, she's not really working. No one should question both the legitimacy and the worth of a woman's—or man's for that matter—work at home, particularly when this involves the care of children.

Nevertheless, here we will simply touch on some of the issues which are central to the marriage/work connection. And the first thing to say is that employment can be very demanding. It can soak up vast amounts of time and energy. While this country was primarily agricultural in its earlier days (which meant that all the family members worked around the home), we are now more of a white- and blue-collar society. This means that employed spouses usually spend at least five days per week away from the home. (An interesting variation is the growing popularity of the practice of telecommuting, where the worker may actually work at home while being electronically connected with offices, factories, clients, etc. by fax, computer and telephone. Of course, this setup causes as many new problems for marriage and family life as it solves.)

Mention, too, must be made of the travel factor involved in commuting across town or across the country. Excessive time away from home can put stress on the marital relationship. Once again, the approach advocated here is to look realistically at your commuting situation, talk about it, relate it to your values and what you want from your life together, and go from there. Too many couples simply wait too long to discuss problems which are related to employment, money, religion and other areas prone to either misunderstanding, hurt feelings or disagreement.

Another area of concern regarding employment is the toll taken by some occupations. Pressure-packed jobs, especially for those who respond to this situation with high stress, often spill over into family life. Bringing home one's work can take two forms. First, actually doing paper work or making phone calls robs a marriage of important time for a couple to be together. Second, dwelling on one's job problems at home can occupy all one's mental space, leaving little energy for spouse or children.

Finally, there is the chronic problem of work overload, which means too much work and not enough time. While it is reasonable to have certain times during the year when one's job requirements increase, if this is a year-round situation there are no winners from a marriage and family perspective.

GETTING STARTED

At one end of the spectrum, the first weeks of marriage can set a new personal level of excitement and joy. At the other end, they can be filled with confusion, questioning, anxiety and worry. Ninety-nine percent of couples fall between the two extremes. A positive experience of the first few weeks is usually determined by the quality of preparations made by the couple. The key is getting to know each other well beyond the level of superficiality. Most of the problems of the first weeks come in a package called "surprise." No one likes surprises, especially in their expectations of marriage.

A certain level of anxiety and frustration at this time is normal, and may be a very good sign, too. Newlyweds should want to please each other and to work at determining what's best for their beloved, themselves and their relationship.

After the wedding day, couples usually go on a honeymoon, which is a very important event. Getting completely away from the observations of others has not only an important physical dimension but also a psychological one. In a sense, the honeymoon is a "clean break" from previous routines and family ties. While it may be only of short duration, it symbolizes the dramatic change from single life to married life. (There is an old joke which contains rich wisdom: "What is a honeymoon salad?" "Let us alone.")

The purpose of the honeymoon is first of all to enjoy each other. This means that it is not a time to cover eight countries in five days nor to join an escorted tour where you are mingling with two hundred or so wonderful people with cameras. It's time for the two of you—no more, no less.

LEARNING TO LIVE TOGETHER

Beginning married life together after the wedding offers new opportunities to love and be loved. Anxious to please each other and perhaps a bit worried about the many details of daily living, couples usually do anything but "settle down" to quiet days and nights together. There's too much electricity in the air.

Sometimes lifelong habits of one or both partners cause tension and irritation. What's particularly distressing is that a couple may be unaware of what's really going on. They may think that "the honeymoon is over" and that they are already "falling out of love," when in reality they are just experiencing the natural process of two relative strangers learning to live together.

There are many potential areas of conflict you should reflect upon: eating habits and table manners, sleeping routines and the temperature of the room, television watching, socializing with neighbors, the use of the telephone, reading and quiet time and the many indirect patterns of communication relating to personal needs, desires and preferences—particularly in the context of sexual activity.

Here are examples of some common situations:

* He thinks that it's wonderful to eat by candlelight each night, but she enjoys having dinner before the television set.

* She likes to gulp an instant breakfast, while he likes a full meal in the morning.

* He thinks it's important to save every penny they can, while she believes that money is meant to be spent.

* She likes to listen to music undisturbed, and he prefers music to be in the background while they do other things.

* A light dusting of the furniture is his idea of housecleaning, but her approach includes shampooing the carpet and repainting the walls.

* She likes pets, while he's allergic to pet hair.

* His usual bedtime is 10:45, while hers is no sooner than midnight.

* She's a floss fanatic, and he's a once-a-day toothbrusher.

You can see that virtually no area of living is exempt from these common personal differences. The first days and weeks of marriage are the time when couples experience them firsthand. It is important not to sweep these little problems under the rug, but it is equally necessary to keep them in perspective. If one of your new spouse's habits is irritating to you, mention it in a nonthreatening way and seek a simple solution. On the other hand, some things you will just have to learn to live with. Remember, you promised to love the other "for better or worse."

PRIVACY

Because married life is about the closest living arrangement available to humans (with the possible exception of a nursing mother with her infant), it may seem to rule out almost all forms of privacy. This is not necessarily true. The question of privacy does merit discussion and accommodation to each other's needs. For example, some people meet their need for privacy while commuting back and forth from their job. Other's do it while taking a slow and reflective bath. Some truly need to read the morning newspaper undisturbed at the breakfast table.

Don't interpret your spouse's desire to be alone as personal rejection. It may be the small bit of time that he or she requires in order to be more fully present to you the rest of the day. Life always seems to require some sort of balance or pressure-release valve, and life in marriage is no exception. Good marriages boast of many satisfying times together, but also of many quiet moments alone.

THE PAYOFF

While you may not believe this, the difficulties and challenges you face in the first year of marriage may make it the hardest, the happiest and the most important year of your married life—all rolled into one. What happens in the first year is that patterns of communication, problem-solving and basic routines are laid in place. Remember, the cement is still moist. While this turmoil can sometimes make you think and feel like you are on an emotional rollercoaster and maybe even cause you to worry, at times, that you might even have made a big mistake in getting married to this person, the first year can also be wonderfully exciting and rewarding.

What can result is a heightened sensitivity to each other and to the marriage. A successful first year can lead to the realization of a deep and intimate marriage, which is among the great treasures available in this life. It can provide you with abiding happiness, profound moments of ecstasy, and a feeling of satisfaction hardly imagined.

With such possibilities for marriage, why is it that marriage receives such a bad rap from so many people? The transition from the "exciting" life of singlehood to that of "boring" marriage is often portrayed as a kind of death sentence. Life ends when marriage begins, these prophets of doom warn.

Perhaps part of the explanation rests in the differences between a self-centered, secular view of marriage and the Christian view, which understands marriage as a privileged way of living Jesus' command to love our neighbor as he loved us.

In one sense, this Christian challenge is born anew with each of us. We are each invited to dedicate full heart, mind and body to the adventure of loving others. In marriage, the shape of the Christian calling is focused on two very special, very different people who are now wife and husband. They are called to climb a difficult mountain, but once the heights have been scaled, they will together be able to see forever.

POINTS FOR REFLECTION

1. Marriages are not destroyed by the mere encounter with rough spots but by the inadequate way couples negotiate them.

2. Your success in marriage will depend on how well you translate inevitable conflict into mutually acceptable solutions.

3. Arguments are simply occasions where the individuality of each marriage partner comes to the surface. A marriage with no arguments may be a marriage where neither party is at home.

4. Some say you can always tell a married couple in a restaurant. They are the ones silently staring at their food.

5. Criticism implies superiority. Persuasion suggests competition. Compromise indicates equality.

QUESTIONS FOR DISCUSSION

1. What customs from your partner's ethnic background do you enjoy? Which ones bother you? What traditions from your own family background do you want to bring into your marriage?

2. What is it about your parents' or your parents-in-law's manner of dealing with conflicts that you don't want to replicate in your marriage?

3. List three things that you're pretty sure you agree upon and three things you think you don't. Now exchange lists and discuss how you are going to resolve any differences.

COMMUNICATION

Communication is as important in marriage as the flow of blood is to your body. Blood brings in nourishment and carries away poisonous wastes. So does communication. Good, supportive words enrich your love, while critical, harmful words tear it apart.

Words said to your spouse have more weight than any other words you express. You have no doubt heard the warning, "Be careful what you say. It could be used against you in court." Well, a similar carefulness about words also applies in marriage. Words are not forgotten. They are stored in the marriage databank each person carries around in his or her head.

Unfortunately, this carefulness can have a negative side. If married couples guard communication between themselves to the degree that only "safe" topics are discussed or only words guaranteed not to cause argument or a negative reaction are said, then their conversation will inevitably become dull and boring. The flow of life between them will be bland and lack nourishment.

MEANING OF WORDS

One of the most difficult aspects of effective communication is that people sometimes use the same words but ascribe different meanings to them. Both assume that the other person knows exactly what's meant, when this is not true. Misunderstanding follows.

Gary, for example, is unwinding after a difficult day at work. While stretched out on the couch, his wife, Ann, leans over to kiss him. "Thanks," he responds, "I really need to be babied tonight." Ann immediately stiffens and quickly goes to the kitchen. Puzzled, Gary wonders whether her abrupt departure was based on something he said. Yet he is confused, because all he said was that he needed to be babied. What's the fuss? After gaining enough courage to ask his wife what happened (always a difficult move), Gary learns that the word "baby" releases a whole flood of negative emotions in her. One of her mother's commonest put-downs was to call her a baby. In her family, that meant she was weak and helpless. When Gary asked to be treated like a baby, Ann became upset—even though he didn't mean it in the same way.

After a minor disagreement with her husband, Joyce jokes the next day on the phone with her best friend about how she and Mike had had a fight. Mike, overhearing the conversation, becomes totally silent and aloof and refuses to even discuss what's bothering him. Later, when he is able to relax a bit, he opens up to her that when she called their argument "a fight," he panicked. When his mom and dad had fights, they often became violent and abusive. Now Mike recognizes his own temper and is always on guard not to get angry. The word "fight" surfaced all these emotions in him, and that's why he retreated.

COMMUNICATING FEELINGS

Feelings are real. Feelings are important. But often we have to guess concerning the feelings of another—even a close friend or a spouse. Some of us are very good at hiding or disguising our feelings. Sometimes, too, people—especially men—have only a fuzzy or general awareness of their own feelings. They have grown so good at ignoring their feelings that it is almost as if the transmitter which sends the "feeling" message to the brain is disconnected.

In either case—whether you can't read the other's feelings or you can't get in touch with your own—nothing gets communicated.

On her way home after losing an important sale which had also prompted criticism from her boss, Maryanne felt irritated and depressed. If she says to her husband, "Dan, I've really had a bad day and I feel real edgy. I need a few minutes to relax and collect myself," things will probably go well. But if she tries to ignore her feelings and attempts to get right to fixing dinner and interacting with her kids, she will quite likely get angry at her family without realizing that the problem may lie elsewhere.

Bob comes home from the factory and notices that Monica, his wife, is upset. He immediately concludes that she is mad at him for stopping off somewhere on the way home. Yet, all kinds of other factors may be at play. Monica may be disturbed because her mother just called and reminded her about her dad's birthday, which she forgot was the day before. Perhaps she was also worried that something might have happened to Bob. If Bob can identify the real cause of Monica's strong feelings, especially the negative ones, he can begin to deal with the real issues, and not with the symptoms.

MEANING OF ACCEPTANCE

Open and nonjudgmental acceptance is a very important part of marital communication. You probably know right away when your partner really wants to hear what you have to say. You can speak easily and freely. You sense a care and concern for your words. Feeling comfortable, you are more easily able to share very personal and important messages.

You may also have been in situations when the other person exhibits a negative and judgmental attitude toward you and you cannot wait to end the conversation. You want to protect yourself against harsh criticism and become defensive and protective. The less you reveal in that situation, the better you feel.

Ideally, marriage is a relationship between two very good friends. Each should value the opinion of the other and not seek to undermine his or her confidence. Nevertheless, such undercutting happens easily in many marriages. Sometimes it's a carry-over from the kinds of communication patterns each individual grew up with, and sometimes it is merely the couple's way of engaging in "the war of the sexes." Good marriages allow each spouse to be vulnerable to the other. They presume acceptance and respect. This opens the door to honesty and a full revealing of each one's thoughts and feelings.

Trying to express your deep feelings is like swimming in a recently thawed lake in early spring. You carefully insert your toe into the water, and, if you survive that first touch, you slowly wade in. If you find your body becoming numb, you head back for the shore and avoid further swimming for quite a while. It's the same when you engage in a conversation with your spouse—you "test the waters" before moving into deeper matters.

There are conversation "starters" and conversation "stoppers." Al tells Jan that he's unhappy with his job. Evaluate the following responses by Jan:

a. *"You certainly shouldn't be satisfied; they're not paying you enough."*

b. *"Oh, I'm not terribly happy with the things I have to do either."*

c. *"Don't start that! We've too many bills to pay for you to start thinking about changing jobs."*

d. *"We all get discouraged. What do you want for supper?"*

e. *"You sound really upset. Tell me a little more."*

Of all these answers, only "e" invites further communication between the couple.

ACCUSATIONS

Maureen tells Frank, "A young man came by selling magazines and . . ." Frank breaks in, "Don't tell me you were taken in by some door-to-door con man!" Maureen immediately sees Frank as a prosecuting attorney and may even lie about the magazines she bought. Next time she will find it a little harder to talk with her husband.

Bill drinks too much and is loud at a party. On the way home, Kate says, "You are a drunken exhibitionist!" Bill is sullen, apologizes, and strikes back. The next day, Kate tries again to express some of her feelings. "I was kind of embarrassed last night, Bill." He responds, "Why?" The path of communication is then reopened. This time, the problem was stated without an accusation.

Sometimes an attack is recognized by the words used: "You jerk!"(You can imagine what follows.) Sometimes the attack is present in the tone of voice. Think of how many different ways the following can be said: "I just love it when you do that!"

Certain trigger phrases carry a hidden accusation which invites a hostile reply. For example:

* "What's wrong with you now?" (Other versions: "There is always something wrong with you. What is it this time?" and "Can't you ever get it right? How many times do I have to tell you?")

* "This is more than I expect from you, but . . ." ("From history, I have learned that you always mess things up, but I will give you one final chance.")

* "How many times do I have to ask you . . . ?" ("Do I have to spell it out for you?" or "I know your sinister plan to frustrate me, but . . .")

How could the following openings possibly be completed in a loving way?

* "Didn't you promise me that you would . . ."
* "What's the use of reminding you that . . ."
* "Where did you even get the idea that . . ."
* "I don't want to complain, but . . ."

So many phrases like the above easily enter conversations between a married couple. They can become habitual, almost taken for granted. But each one in its own way, little by little, cuts into a relationship. Hidden in each are putdowns, criticisms, cynicism, and implications of blame, guilt, or even shame.

NONVERBAL COMMUNICATION

A few years back, a respected anthropologist published an eye-opening book called *The Silent Language*. His main point was that the way we hold our body, the look in our eye and the gestures of our hands all "speak" something. In marriage, couples become astute translators of each other's silent language. "Why are you looking at me that way? What's on your mind?" they'll say. Lack of eye-contact and bodily posture often speak volumes to a spouse.

How does communication occur when there are no words at all? A husband nosily bangs dishes in the sink to let his wife know that he is upset. A wife buries her head in a book or magazine to indicate that she doesn't even want to be in the same room as her husband. Movements as simple as how one turns over in bed invite all kinds of speculation on the part of a sensitive spouse as to what's really going on with his or her partner.

Sometimes body language speaks more directly and honestly than do words. "How are you doing?" asks the wife as she sorts the dirty laundry. "I'm just fine," responds her husband. But his edgy voice, rigid stance and tightly clenched hands tells her he is really not telling her the truth.

TOUCH

A special form of nonverbal communication is touch. Touching another person can signal everything from love to hate, from support to destruction. It can call forth strong emotions and reactions. Someone once answered the question, "What is the most important sex organ?" with the response, "Our skin." And it can be.

A loving, intimate touch is one of the most powerful forms of communication in marriage. At its best, a sexual embrace can truly say something that is beyond words.

With our current awareness of the widespread presence of sexual abuse, however, it helps to be aware of some of the potential implications of this tragedy on a marriage. First, one of the main reasons for the destructive side of sexual abuse is that it is so often brought upon a young person who is largely defenseless. What usually happens in sexual abuse is that an adult crosses the natural boundaries of the child and invades his or her space. Once inside that space, the adult "communicates" largely by touching the child. The child experiences a sense of violation, a kind of unlawful entry. Usually, then, the child creates a strong defense against touch so that no one else may enter. This high wall of protection can be taken into adulthood, making it difficult if not impossible for another adult to touch the abused person, even if the touch is good and desirable.

Reflecting on the destructiveness of the inappropriate use of touch should alert us to its power for harm. Yet it should also help us respect its power for good. In marriage, the loving and respectful use of touch can be one of the richest aspects of married love.

TIMING

The perfect delivery of the punch line by a comedian is a work of art. And when any of the great ones are asked their secret, they all say the same thing, "Timing is everything." It is the same with good communication. There is a time to communicate and a time to be quiet in marriage; a time to speak and a time to listen. The emotional mood of both partners often affects whether the timing is right or not.

Stress, fatigue, tension, the grips of a terrible headache, or just the common cold all influence us in ways not conducive to good communication. And even more problematic are the barriers caused by one or both partners' use of excessive amounts of alcohol or drugs.

Sometimes it is helpful for a couple to get away from familiar settings (and the reminders of work undone) in order to communicate clearly and lovingly. Many couples enjoy walking and talking. Sometimes a drive in the country can ease the flow of words. Finding time to talk together about the more serious things in your life is important. Put it in your schedule, lest it slip into that mounting pile of "things to be done" that never are.

FIGHTING FAIR

A very effective "dirty tactic" in marital fighting is the silent treatment. The sound of a spouse's total silence can be devastating, since it can often be interpreted as complete rejection. A person who is the victim of the silent treatment can only turn inward and become depressed or turn outward in harshness and even violence. Each partner, whether feeling hurt, angry, frustrated, frightened or vengeful, must keep in mind the drastic effect that the unwarranted cold shoulder can have on the future of a relationship.

On the other hand, it may be necessary to lower the temperature a bit when discussion gets too heated, when emotions block thought, or when winning the argument becomes the only goal. Many arguments occur when only two seemingly conflicting options, his or hers, are on the table. When stress and anxiety get heavy, the possibility of bringing in a third, a fourth, or even a fifth option is ruled out. Creativity rarely happens while people are shouting.

Here are some simple guidelines for fighting fair and arguing successfully. First, stay focused on the topic or issue at hand. Don't dig up old bones from the past. Marriage is not intended as warfare, so the amount of ammunition you can keep stored in your memory is of no use. Sorry. The goal of communication in marriage is not to win, but to walk away with both of you happy, satisfied and fully functioning.

Second, watch language which unnecessarily heats up the room. Name calling only puts the other person into a defensive or hostile mood. *Listen before you speak.* Don't assume you know what the other person is thinking or feeling. Hear him or her out. Explore options. He wants to have a big party. She wants to have the couple next door over for a quiet dinner. Think of another option. Encourage the next door neighbors to have a big party!

GUNNY-SACKING

Why people don't say what they should say when it's best to say it is a mystery of the human species. Nevertheless, some people store up complaints, drag them around in a sack, and when the sack just gets too heavy or too full . . . well, you have an incident like the one experienced by Eileen.

Eileen got home from work forty-five minutes late one night. George, her husband, exploded in a burst of fury way out of proportion to the simple inconvenience caused by Eileen's tardiness. Why? Well, while she was in transit to home, he had been mentally rehearsing his opening lines about some simple issue. The later she became, the longer he had to dig into the "gunny-sack" of complaints that he had been saving for just this kind of moment. Eileen walked in the door, and whammo! She was "gunny- sacked."

You can easily understand, objectively, why the practice of "gunny-sacking" is ineffective and often quite damaging. Therefore, this is a good time for both of you to vote against it happening in your marriage. Talk about matters when they are still current news. Clear them up soon so that they don't grow into mountains. Occasional confrontations are a healthy sign of life and love in a marriage. Certainly they are to be preferred over the artificial calm which prevails when there is a room full of filled gunny-sacks waiting to detonate.

NAGGING

Here is a dictionary-like description of nagging: to annoy by continual fault-finding, scolding, complaining and urging. And while you won't find this statement in the dictionary, it might as well be there: nagging never works. Nagging is a habit people adopt when they are not getting what they want. They decide to wear down other people to their point of view. If agreement is eventually gotten, however, it is always seasoned with resignation and resentment.

Nagging often comes from deep, unresolved issues in a marriage. Something is missing in the relationship. If you find yourself moving into a nagging mode, try to learn what's really bothering you and deal with that—instead of driving your partner crazy over something that neither of you cares that much about anyway.

A NOTE ON MARRIAGE COUNSELING

Sometimes you can be so close to a problem that you can't see it. Sometimes your emotions get to such a level that you can't think with much clarity. Sometimes you just get stuck and you need a push. If we're talking about cars, it's wise to see a good mechanic. If we're talking about marriage, it's often good to seek the guidance of a trained marriage counselor.

Marriage is a very complicated human arrangement. Sorting out what's happening between a wife and husband, especially in those areas of which they are largely unaware, can take the skills of a caring outsider. Counselors provide insight into what's going on in a marriage. You know intimately only your own marriage and possibly that of your parents. Expert counselors know of hundreds of marriages and have seen firsthand the many patterns, both healthy and unhealthy, that marriages develop. They can alert you to influences from your personal history which may be at work in your marriage. They can suggest better ways to communicate with each other. They can serve as touchstones that can help you resolve your differences.

No longer is it considered a stigma to visit a counselor. In truth, it may well be a sign of your common sense to seek help early for unresolved issues in your relationships. Most counselors will tell you that they love to work with married couples in situations where they are not yet at the stage of separation or divorce. In other words, they enjoy supplying people with preventative medicine rather than embalming fluid. Some marriage experts recommend that couples visit a counselor for a regular check-up in much the same way you would see a doctor every few years or bring in your car at 50,000 miles.

If you ever feel you need to see a counselor, ask around for recommendations. Many states require the licensing of counselors for the protection of the clients. Often local clergy are, or know of, good counselors. Your marriage is a living thing. Care for it and nurture it so that it remains healthy indefinitely.

(P.S. If one of you really feel you need to see a counselor and your partner doesn't, go by yourself. A good counselor will help you sort out your feelings and, if necessary, help you develop a strategy for getting your spouse to come with you.)

POINTS FOR REFLECTION

1. It's not always what you say but the way you say it that hurts.

2. Keep a mental scorecard on how often you use "should" or "ought" with your partner, and—after you become aware of this practice—end it.

3. Lack of communication can extend eventually to every area of your relationship: important beliefs, deep values, vital interests and all the other major issues involved in two people trying to forge a life together.

4. One of the most disheartening moments in a marriage is when you learn that your partner is not really interested in what you say.

5. Too much talk on your part may mean that you are not listening very well. God gave each person two ears and one mouth.

QUESTIONS FOR DISCUSSION

1. How did your parents communicate with each other. What did they talk about? How was conflict handled in your home?

2. Recall your communication patterns during your courtship. Did you experience nagging, gunnysacking, the cold shoulder or silent treatment, digging up old bones? How might you break any bad habits you have developed?

3. What are your current thoughts about counseling?

The lithe, handsome youth ran swiftly over the fields to the dwelling of his beloved. He knocked vigorously, and to her question, "Who is it?" he cried, "It is thy lover!" The door remained barred. Crestfallen, he withdrew to meditate.

Hours later at evening he returned, this time to tap gently at the door. When her question came again, "Who is it?" he whispered, "It is thyself!" and was immediately admitted to her embrace.

Arabian Legend

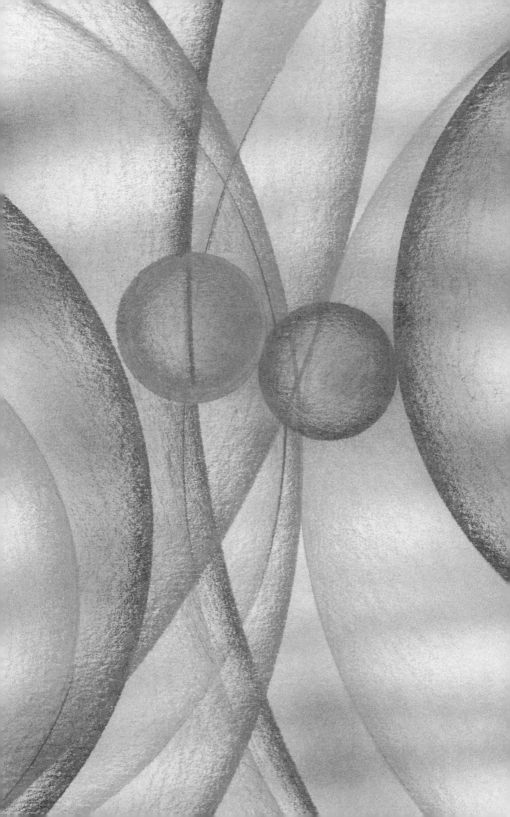

SEXUALITY AND SENSUALITY

We live in a time when everyone's personal ideas about religion and politics are his or her own. Independent thinking in both areas is encouraged and accepted. Can the same be said about our views on human sexuality?

It would seem not. People today seem to be aligned into two camps on the issue of sex, one conservative and the other liberal, with both pretty intolerant of the other. Yet the truth is that sexuality (and its "cousin" sensuality) is a complex, difficult, powerful and exciting matter that is not conducive to simple solutions or "sound bite" slogans.

THE "NUPTIAL MEANING OF THE BODY"

Healthy sexuality and sensuality are significant aspects of marriage. Often the early attraction between a woman and a man are filled with thoughts and feelings with sexual overtones. While you are in the midst of this excitement, it may be surprising to learn that, while sex can certainly be fun and enjoyable, it can also become a problem in marriage. God did not necessarily intend it that way, but we humans have a way of messing up what was originally good. Still, here's an important starting point for our discussion of sexuality and marriage: God created sex and blessed it as good.

For at least three decades, we have been in the middle of what is sometimes called the "sexual revolution." Its basic rallying cry was the liberating of our sexuality from what was judged confining and restrictive in the past. It seems that no segment of society was exempted from this movement. From a positive perspective, the sexual revolution has resulted in a greater openness about sex and in a general agreement on the fundamental goodness and value of our sexuality for both women and men.

We have also learned that our sexuality is a powerful part of our personality. Sex is not only something we do; sex is something we are. Sexuality influences our thoughts, feelings and behavior, and even spills over into our basic beliefs and values. In fact, the integrating of love, trust and commitment into our sexuality is what truly humanizes it.

In the book of Genesis, the creation of human sexuality happens automatically, as soon as man and woman are created. Once we go from one to two in the garden, we discover sex. In the writings of Pope John Paul II, we find many references to the fact that "written" in our bodies is a message from God that women and men are created to be with and for each other. He calls this the "nuptial meaning of the body."

So, sex is with us because God made us that way. But we are also challenged to discover its deepest meaning. If we do, we learn that sexuality carries with it the power to develop the love between a married couple and a power to embody their love in new life.

Sexuality can serve human growth and the attainment of intimacy, but only if it incorporates the God-given values which were part of its original creation. If sexuality is used to control, hurt, or manipulate others, if it is depersonalized and severed from its connection to the expression of deeply committed love and fruitfulness, it loses its power for good.

CONFRONTING OUR SEXUALITY

We live in an image-filled world. Products are advertised and packaged with images intended to draw attention to their presence. The association of sex with all kinds of nonsexual items demonstrates how sex gains meaning by association. For example, sex is blended with violence in many music videos. Sex is associated with fun and youth in beer commercials. Sex is connected with the fast life in automobile commercials.

Media stars today are packaged in much the same way. Many use various types of sexually-related imagery to augment their public identities. Let's face it, the use of sex gets attention.

Perhaps the most degrading use of sex is related to the abuse of another person to fulfill one's private "needs," as in prostitution or sexual abuse. Sadly, many of these "needs" are less than human and result in the degradation of defenseless women and children.

Yet our sexuality and the desires associated with it have a proper and beneficial place in human life, specifically inside of marriage. Sex is a gift from God, who entrusts us with using it so that we can create life in abundance—both between us and from us.

MALE AND FEMALE

At the moment of your conception, your path toward being either a female or a male was established. You now are composed of about three billion cells, and every single cell of "you" is either female or male. Gender identity is a biochemical given, and your personality reflects this foundation. While we now know of some very occasional exceptions to clear sexual typing, virtually the entire population is either female or male.

Besides having this biological foundation to our sexuality, we are taught from our earliest days how to act in accord with our gender. An exciting feature of today's culture has been a loosening of rigid sexual roles, which has allowed both men and women to chose interests and even careers more freely and independently. Our language has tried to keep pace with this openness. We now speak of "firefighters" instead of "firemen," or "mail carriers" in place of "mailmen." Perhaps the most important shift has taken place within the family itself, where the nurturing of children is now done much more jointly by both fathers and mothers.

On the other hand, the erosion of rigid sexual roles and behavior has created some anxiety between the sexes. When women and men could simply adopt preexisting roles and wear them like suits of clothes, life seemed easier and less complicated. Now the determination of gender attitudes and behavior is largely left to each individual.

Still, there remains sexual differences which are profound, and, let's not forget, make life more interesting. Studies in learning and thought patterns, ways of relating to each other, and approaches to problem-solving still show different tendencies between women and men. Men, for example, usually seem to be more goal-oriented, while woman appear very sensitive to process or the way one gets to a goal. In general, men are more focused on work and career, while woman are more sensitive to personal relationships. While it is almost impossible to set down a list of differences which are without exception, it is safe to conclude that there remain important distinctions between the male and female of our species and that these differences are worked out best through the interaction between a particular woman and a particular man. This process helps create the tension that makes people want to get together, get to know each other, and—sometimes and eventually—get married.

SEXUAL ATTRACTION

There is a biological basis underneath the notion of becoming "turned on" in the presence of a person of the opposite sex whom one finds attractive. Actual chemical changes in the body cause emotional responses which at times can be quite intense. While the research in this area notes that such intensity is difficult to sustain over the long run, it plays an important role in the early phases of dating, courtship and marriage.

What's also important to be aware of is the fact that this physical and emotional reaction is not simply restricted to one's first love or the love which leads to marriage. It can reappear at other times in life and sometimes creates a situation when personal discipline needs to be exercised.

It might be said that sexual attraction energizes us to take the risk of the deeper relationship of marriage. This very natural reaction of one human being to another is meant to bring two people closer together in a union that is physical, psychological, intellectual and spiritual.

Sexual desire not only leads to the formation of a special relationship between a couple, it also contributes to the growth of their love. In a human and Christian sense, sexual enjoyment between a married couple is part of the overall process of their getting to know each other more completely. Their sexuality plays a major role in the happiness they discover in each other and in their marriage.

VARIETIES OF SEXUAL EXPERIENCE

Like most of our biologically based experiences—for example eating and drinking—sexuality can be connected to a whole set of meanings. Sexual activity can be joyful, exciting, passionate, boring, matter-of-fact, and even at times a chore. (Believe it or not!) It can be used to give support or love to another. But it can also be reduced to enslavement, punishment, control and manipulation. In and of itself, sex is always ambiguous. It depends on the whens, hows, whys, and with whoms to give it a meaning.

We communicate through our sexuality. Just as we employ verbal and nonverbal language in interacting with others, so do we also use sexual language. Our sexual language is aptly designed to communicate strong feelings and convictions of love. It is not the only language of love, yet it is a very important one in a marriage.

Physically expressing love to a person of the other sex befits so beautifully the life of the married. It is lovemaking without holding back, a love of letting go, a love of vulnerability, a love with an open-ended future. The law of sexual fidelity in marriage is not something that is given to the married as a restriction or as a burden. It Is actually a freeing up of each person to fully relate sexually, without fear of rejection or betrayal. With the reality of AIDS and other sexually transmitted diseases, sexual fidelity is also a promise to your spouse that you would never risk having the act of love become a source of harm in your marriage.

Sexual love in marriage also has a procreative dimension. Here again, it is the nature of the love itself which gives meaning to the sexual act of intercourse. It is as if a couple's love for each other cannot be contained and overflows to create new life. The first "fruit" of married love is the child which is born of their sexual union. In a way, married couples imitate the love of God by creating a new life.

God's love overflowed and creation came into existence. Our parents loved, and they joined with God in bringing new life into the world. That is why the word "procreation" most adequately describes human conception and birth. We are created from the love of God and from the love of our parents. Much less appropriate, although widely used, is the more depersonalized word "reproduction." We should not come off an assembly line in a laboratory. We should all be created out of love. For this reason, the Church has been critical of some of the more "modern" methods of reproduction.

FEMALE PROCREATIVE SYSTEM

At about eleven or twelve years of age, a young girl's pituitary gland in the brain secretes hormones which initiate important changes in her reproductive system. Her ovaries begin to ovulate and her uterus begins to create the rich lining needed to receive the ovum. With fertilization not taking place, her uterus goes through the natural process each month of expelling its unused lining, and menstruation begins.

Each egg or ovum contains the full genetic package of the woman. She will continue to ovulate about once a month until she reaches menopause in her forties or fifties (although there are many variations to this cycle depending on the individual woman and sometimes upon circumstances of her life). Knowledge of the unique cycle of each woman is important if a couple intends on practicing natural family planning methods, either to have a child or to postpone pregnancy.

One of the wondrous miracles of God's creation is the biological system designed to bring new life into the world. As you know, the first "home" of the new life is the mother's uterus. While there, the growing person is nourished by the body of its mother. Modern science has demonstrated the importance of a mother caring for her own body during pregnancy. Unhealthy substances like addictive drugs, alcohol, nicotine and even over-the-counter medicines can be harmful to the dependent person growing within.

The lower end of the uterus opens onto a muscular canal called the vagina. It is this external opening which receives semen from the penis of the male and which provides the opening through which will pass a developed fetus at birth. The opening of the vagina is covered with two layers of skin called the labia. At the top of the labia is a small organ called the clitoris. This organ has nerve endings which are quite sensitive to tactile stimulation.

The entrance to the vagina is partially covered by a thin membrane called the hymen. Prior to first sexual intercourse, this membrane is usually closed, so gentleness by the partner is important. Rigorous physical activity during adolescence can also open the hymen, however, disproving the myth that if it is open the woman must have had previous sexual relations. Upon first intercourse, the woman may experience pressure and even some bleeding. This is normal. Should penetration prove quite difficult or painful, a physician should be consulted.

A woman is fertile for only a short time during her menstrual cycle. More information about determining whether a woman is infertile or fertile can be obtained by becoming familiar with recent scientific methods for interpreting the symptoms or signs of ovulation. Experienced and trained married couples, along with local physicians familiar with natural family planning, should be consulted to learn these new findings. The correct use of natural family planning methods has helped many married couples exercise their God-given responsibility in procreating new life. Despite popular opinion, which often takes the form of ridicule, natural family planning is not only a practical and safe form of birth control, it can also serve to strengthen the marital relationships by encouraging mutual sensitivity, communication and respect between wife and husband.

MALE PROCREATION SYSTEM

Boys enter puberty at about twelve or thirteen. Their testicles begin producing sperm, which are the male contribution to the procreative process. The sperm are deposited through the erect penis within the female vagina during sexual intercourse. The size of the male penis has no effect on either the pleasure associated with intercourse or the capacity to procreate. In some instances, males may have a low sperm count. If a married couple experience infertility, this should be checked by medical tests.

Sexual arousal in males and females is similar but somewhat different. Usually, the male is more quickly aroused, while the female is more responsive to longer "foreplay." The male may at times ejaculate prior to inserting his penis into the vagina. Such "premature ejaculation" is usually a matter of overexcitement or lack of experience and will stop once a couple becomes more comfortable with each other. If the problem persists, however, the man should discuss the problem with his doctor.

PHYSIOLOGY OF SEX IN MARRIAGE

Human sexuality, while it is founded on the biological sexual differences between women and men, draws its meaning from the whole life of love between wife and husband. When asked the moment their sexual lovemaking begins, many wise married couples are apt to respond, "In the kitchen, when dinner is being prepared or the dishes are being washed." Their point is simple: marital sexuality cannot be reduced to the activities of the bedroom. It is a daylong and lifelong process.

The physiological aspect, however, remains important. This is not so much a matter of following a "recipe book" of sexual instructions as it is a matter of honest communication and attentiveness between the wife and husband.

Each partner in a marriage will have his or her own preferences and ways in which he or she enjoys expressing love. Sensitivity to each other's likes and dislikes is very important. So, too, is consideration of the "nontechnical" aspects of sex, for example, the degree of privacy desired, the time of day preferred, the amount of "romance" appreciated, and the overall health or emotional condition of each party.

Sexual arousal is a very complex process for both wife and husband, but probably more so for the wife. People differ in terms of sexual desire, and while most will say that the male has a greater interest in sex, this cannot be thought of as a universal law. Likewise, it is generally true that it will take longer for a woman than a man to be aroused to the point when sexual climax can occur. Here again, communication between the couple is helpful.

When both partners are "ready," the man inserts his penis into the woman's vagina. Both then engage in bodily movement which increases contact and friction and which eventually results in climax by the male as he ejaculates the seminal fluid into the vagina. Female climax may occur at the same time as the male's, or it may happen before or after. Upon climax, there normally follows a feeling of relaxation, espe cially for the male. Mutual sensitivity at this point is especially important, because a man upon climaxing may consider sexual activity over and no longer remain aware of the desires of the woman.

It should be noted that both the wife and the husband have an equal right to the enjoyment and benefits which come from the sexual aspect of their marriage. From time to time, their interests and capacity to respond may be different. Some women experience their sexuality differently depending on which part of their monthly cycle they are in. Outside stress and pressures (job, children, illness) can affect both partners.

While the sexual aspect of marriage is important, couples who benefit the most from it seem to be those who do not take it all that seriously. They bring a playful and joyful attitude to their sexual love. Their sexuality as much celebrates their love as it contributes to its deepening.

With recent awareness of the high incidence of sexual abuse and even incest in childhood, it should be mentioned that the effect of this can carry over into marriage. To sum up briefly, inappropriate sexual activity cannot but affect its participants. Since sexuality is at the center of our beings, bad experiences will produce negative effects. To protect themselves against further harm, individuals who have been abused often create barriers to sexual intimacy. Their defensiveness can surface even in a loving marriage. It is up to the spouse in such a situation to be especially sensitive and for both partners to seek the advice and counseling they need to overcome the effects of this great evil.

SPIRITUALITY OF SENSUALITY

Read sometime the book in the Bible called the Song of Songs. You may be surprised at the candor with which the physical love between wife and husband is described. Biblical scholars today point out that the book really is a collection of Jewish wedding songs which were sung or recited at wedding feasts. They are quite sensual and, to some minds, might appear inappropriate to have been included in a collection of inspired sacred writings.

In fact, for much of Christian history these verses were judged to be merely poetic descriptions of the soul's relationship to God. It was thought that God could not really be interested in the details of human, physical, sexual love. Today, with the insights of biblical scholarship, we are able to read these descriptions in the more literal way they were intended and to see in them the true message of the Bible: that God created us with sensual bodies and that we are to enjoy them as part of God's good creation.

Thus, the discovery of each other's bodies is very much a part of the sacramental dimension of marriage. Marriage partners can become for each other a special way in which God's love is experienced. We can now speak of a "spirituality of sensuality" without blushing or apology. Married couples can come to know the presence of the loving God in the very act of becoming "one flesh."

JOYS OF SEXUALITY

While you could learn how to engage in sexual relations from instructions printed on one 3x5 card, it would take volumes to show you how to combine sexuality with true love. Getting to love each other sexually will be a lifelong learning experience. It will take care, patience and gentleness of spirit.

If one or both of you come to the topic of sexuality with cautiousness and timidity, it does not mean that you are not gifted with a rich sexuality. As was already mentioned, our sexuality is connected with the deepest part of our humanity. We must be careful that we don't minimize its importance by approaching it trivially or mechanically. Good sex can be rich with human meaning.

To keep the sexual aspect of marriage alive and well requires imagination and creativity. Most human activities can be ruined by routine, and sex is no exception. Lovemaking that is too patterned and rigid can make sexual relations dull. Like all the other important areas of your marriage, it's important to invest time, energy and even study into making your sexual life an important part of your lives together.

ATMOSPHERE AND CONTENT

The emotional or psychological "setting" in which sex is

experienced in marriage contributes a lot to its total meaning. The time of day, the lighting, music, scented candles all can endow the moment of encounter with a romantic spirit.

The events just preceding its initiation also affect sex. For example, a day spent in working closely together to accomplish an important task, or, conversely, a day spent in conflict can result in especially meaningful—or especially uncomfortable—sexual activity. Again, it is impossible to establish fixed rules concerning these matters. For one couple, it may be quite destructive to engage in sexual relations after a major argument, but for another it may be the perfect thing to do to bring about reconciliation.

Know for sure, however, that the sexual act cannot be isolated from what happens before or after. It is always part of other things. By the way, that is one of the reasons the best overall setting for lovemaking is committed marriage.

TALK: DURING AND ABOUT

What about talking, or whispering what used to be called "sweet nothings," into the ear of one's beloved in the midst of sexual activity? Again, no fixed rule is available. The best advice is to discuss with each other how you feel about talking while making love. The important thing is to do what comes naturally to the two of you. Remember that sexual activity is symbolic language in itself, and sometimes it may be helpful just to keep quiet and listen to the language of sex.

Should your sexual activity become a problem, however, it is certainly worthy of discussion—preferably away from the bedroom. Many people have grown up in families where such things were never discussed. But sharing of even the most intimate and personal thoughts and feelings should be part of marriage. It's absolutely necessary for successful and satis-fying sexual love for both partners.

FREQUENCY AND DURATION

One important and absolute rule applies to the ideal amount of sex for the typical marriage. The rule is this: Together you decide. What's always important about sex in marriage is that the sexual life of the couple be owned by both of them. Through an understanding of each other's tempera-ment and desires, through an honest analysis of their lifestyle, and through an appreciation of the basic goodness of sexual-ity from a Christian perspective, each couple can and should responsibly and lovingly "work it out."

Remember too, *your* relationship is the only thing to be considered—not any national "averages" or what sexual customs you imagine to be in vogue at the time. In this sense, sex is too important to be left up to outside "experts." Be sensitive to each other. Find out what each of your sexual needs are. Invite, but don't force.

TECHNIQUES

Good knowledge of the physiology of both sexes is important for both partners. Ignorance is the foundation of fear. Fear leads to anxiety. Anxiety often leads to poor performance. And poor performance can lead to frustration.

If in doubt about your partner's feelings or reactions during sex, please ask. It can be a very loving thing to do. Most bookstores contain publications which are guides to better lovemaking.

Slavish following of these so-called "sex manuals," how-ever, opens the door to an impersonal, too self-centered approach to lovemaking. In other words, buyer beware. Nevertheless, many couples can profitably use imaginative suggestions which may help the sexual aspect of their love life. In the end, though, the best source of information is you, both of you. Don't be afraid to be creative and try new things. Remember: You're making *love.*

SOME OLD MYTHS

1. Sex is evil.

   While we know that sexuality is part of God's good creation, its perversion in today's pluralis-tic world can easily bring individuals to think quite differently. Sex is good, but it can be horribly misused. Only when that happens can we think of it as evil. It is not sex that is evil, however. Rather, the evil comes from those who destroy its beauty by using it in ways God did not intend.

2. Knowledge of sex and masculinity go hand in hand.

   For too long it was assumed that men know about "these things" and women do not. In fact sex, like other aspects of life, needs to be learned by everyone. It's not a sign of weak-ness to admit you don't know something. It is a sign of weakness, however, not to have the courage to ask when you are in the dark. That goes for men as well as women.

3. There is a male and a female attitude and response to lovemaking.

There *are* differences between women and men. But what's misleading regarding sex is an easy and simplistic description of what is appropriate to each. Personal history plays a major role in affecting one's capacity for intimacy, which is part of everyone's sexual interest and response. The old myth that men are very interested in sex and women are not can be a dangerous stereo-type. The rule to remember is to talk it over.

4. Intense, simultaneous orgasm is the ideal.

Yes, if a couple experiences orgasm at the same time, it's great. But, if they don't, that's OK too. Sex is not performed for a scorecard or on a rating scale. It is designed to bring two loving spouses closer together and to provide the best of all settings for new life to be brought into the world. Orgasm is the frosting on the cake.

5. The sex act is complicated.

There are two ways in which the deep joy of sexuality can be missed. They are at two extremes. At one end are those who say that the sex act is the most important experience of life. It must, therefore, be approached with great seriousness, and failure to achieve the fullness of sexual possibilities amounts to a disaster. At the other end are those who claim that sex is merely another daily function, like eating lunch, or watching TV, or taking a bath. Pleasant, but no big deal. For these people, sex is trivialized.

In the middle are those who appreciate and respect sexuality as an important part of marriage but not the essence of marriage. For these people, sex takes on its deepest meaning when it is connected with a couple's committed love, their care for each other, and even their love of God.

WONDER OF SEXUALITY

One of the great words of the English language is "awe." It is that special response which arises in us when we are in the presence of beauty and wonder. Awe allows us to appreciate and not to try to control or change that which is there. The appropriate human response when in awe is gratitude. This was what was in the minds of the couple who said to each other on their wedding night:

In this most intimate and private of human acts, we reveal ourselves to each other, we give ourselves to each other, we join our excited bodies and soaring spirits—our lives and our beings—in passion and joy. In this bed, today and through a thousand tomorrows, we dramatize and celebrate our pledge, our willingness to serve, give pleasure, nurture, and heal each other—now and forever.

POINTS FOR REFLECTION

1. Sex is the only biological activity that requires another person for its complete expression and fulfillment.

2. It is impossible to be totally spontaneous when another person is involved. Be open to both the "yes" and the "not now, but later."

3. The sex act is not in itself an act of love. It only becomes loving when connected with other acts of love which go before and after its enactment.

4. Time, not technique, is the key to sexual happiness. Give yourselves time to learn how to be more tender, more responsive, and more patient with each other. All this will make you both more sexy.

5. Sexual intercourse is a special language which can say "I love you" in a way no other can match.

QUESTIONS FOR DISCUSSION

1. What turns you on sexually? What did you find most attractive in your partner when you first met? How does he or she liked to be shown affection?

2. What traits do you consider most "masculine?" Which are most "feminine?" What do you think about the theory that all of us are partly masculine and partly feminine?

3. Express some of the fears you have in the area of sexuality. Do you have any "nightmares" about the future of your sexual life together?

PARENTING

The decision to have a child in today's world is a major one for a married couple. It is an act of faith in the world of tomorrow. Responsible parents-to-be know that there is much more to having children than just delivering a baby. It is also a commitment to raising those children until they are able to live on their own and to caring about them for the rest of their lives. Because of the tremendous stress placed on economics these days, one of the first questions young couples ask is fairly simple: "Can we afford to have a baby?" While having children is certainly a question involving dollars and cents, it is also about values, lifestyles, and religious beliefs.

Many of life's greatest joys are tied to having children. There is the exhilaration of birth and the early days of infant care; the thrill of watching your own child take his or her first steps; the countless moments of satisfaction found in adventuring with one's own child into the magnificent world of God's incredible creation.

Most parents note the rich feeling which comes from communicating their beliefs, values and ideals to a child. And, while no parent ever claims that the task of bringing up a child today is easy, most say that it is well worth the effort.

SHOULD YOU HAVE CHILDREN?

By its very nature, conjugal or married love is doubly creative: It calls forth the fullest development of wife and husband as distinctive feminine and masculine images of God; and it produces, through the creation of a child, a captivating, living symbol of their love.

Contemporary emphasis on the developing happiness of the married couple and their enrichment through the days and nights of married life is long overdue. Their love for each other, however, need not be thought of as competitive to the love they might have for possible children of their union. The "us or them" scenario need not develop. Ideally, a couple will experience their love for each other overflowing into love for new life. Having children is not so much a biological necessity as it is a step in the direction of maturing love.

No one can argue that children are not a burden. But all burdens are not bad. Most everything truly worthwhile in life comes with a price. The extra effort drawn from us in carrying a burden contributes to the very process of our personal deepening. Those who live life without giving of themselves in some way will usually remain at an almost infantile, self-centered stage of human growth. They never know the joy of giving, the sense of self-satisfaction that one has contributed to creating a better world for everyone.

In earlier times, it was not uncommon to hear that one should produce all the children one could. Parental generosity was demonstrated by the abundance of their children. "Families of the Year" were usually those who had a houseful of children. Today, part of the decision to have children also includes choosing when it is best to have them and how many to have. Later, we will discuss Christian reasons for this choice, but here we want to simply state that "more does not necessarily mean better."

Current psychological theory also notes the importance of procreation or fruitfulness during the course of life. In religious terms, you might reflect on the simple phrase, "You were put here for a reason." Many married couples conclude that part of the reason for their lives is to pass life on to others.

EXCUSES, EXCUSES

Some couples say, "We can't bring children into a world like this." It is certainly obvious to everyone that there are major problems in the world today—including overpopulation in some countries. Nevertheless, even a brief study will confirm that history is more like a circle than a straight line when it comes to problems. Health care is a good example. A hundred years ago, many of the diseases which were the big "killers" were defeated by vaccines and other drugs. Now, a new set of diseases creates fear about the future. Yet it is entirely possible that a century from now there will be cures for cancer, heart disease, Alzheimer's, and even AIDS. Yet a new list of ailments may then be confronting humanity.

From a Christian perspective, however, we must always live in the season of hope. The Lord of History is God's Spirit, present and active among us. Before his ascension, Jesus promised not to leave us orphans. This promise holds for us personally and for those whom we bring into the world.

Another excuse some couples give is the money issue. Children, they say, are very expensive. No one—least of all those with children—can argue against that. The federal government likes to estimate the cost of raising children up to their eighteenth birthday. It's always a rough guess, because each family is different as to their lifestyle. Still, the costs these days to raise one child is said to be over $100,000—and that doesn't even count trying to send him or her to college!

Facing that figure in one lump sum would be staggering to say the least. But the "cost" is actually spread out in "not-so-easy daily payments." Confronting this economic reality, however, does allow couples to clarify their values.

REWARDS OF PARENTING

Most parents will say that their children give them much more than they give their children. This happens, however, only when parents themselves are giving people. Parents who use children to fulfill their personal needs soon learn that they aren't getting much out of the experience.

Children are God's way of encouraging a parent to be altruistic, generous and giving. The very structure of the parent-child relationship invites this. Some will say that parental love is most like the love God has for each of us. It is complete giving.

Children also allow parents to relive the times of their own childhood. Parents can relearn from their children the sense of wonder they may have lost along the way. Parents can also learn from their kids how to play again (an experience often in short supply in "serious" adulthood).

Children are also a way in which parents can find their way

in society. Children can provide the opportunity for getting to know neighbors, for example. Adding the role of parent to that of wife or husband opens one to a whole new set of joys, exciting activities, and moments of appreciation and satisfaction.

While you can never expect your love to be returned in exactly the same measure or way that you give it, one of the special joys of parenting is the rich mutual exchange of care and concern that happens between child and parent. Love is not a thing subject to calculation. If you try to measure it, you will be disappointed. Nevertheless, when the love is real and healthy, it will provide parents with unparalleled pleasure.

TRIALS OF PARENTING

When parents gather at parties, it is not long before they begin talking about their kids. Not long into the conversation, one parent will confess how hard parenting is. The rest will knowingly nod. "It's true," they echo. "Children can be a real pain!"

Children take time, patience and money. If they are like most kids, they will break your heart once or twice along the way. Which leads to the first important piece of parental wisdom: Be sure to take care of yourself, too.

The demands of parenting are best responded to when there are two parents, a mom and a dad, who work together as a team. This is the ideal, and even most single parents will agree. The task of working together as parents can also have the added benefit of bringing the parents closer together. Parenting is more an art than a science. The ongoing conversations, the adjustments and negotiation of viewpoints, and even the "taking turns" in feeding a hungry infant or waiting up for a tardy teenager all contribute to the building up of a couple's love for each other and for their children.

One of the best social trends today is captured in a subtle shift in language. In former times, most discussion of child-rearing focused almost exclusively on the role of the mother. Dad slayed the dragons that were outside the family home, while mom nurtured the life of the children within. Now we speak of "parenting" rather than just "mothering." This change relates to our growing appreciation of the role of both parents.

FAMILY PLANNING

From our current knowledge of biology, we know that most couples are capable of producing many offspring—in most cases more than a couple could possibly care for responsibly. Therefore, while generosity in procreating is a value, it must also be related to other values. For instance, parents have a clear responsibility to the children who are already a part of their family. They also have a duty to their own relationship, to parents and other relatives, and to society in general. Sometimes for family, personal or economic reasons, couples decide that it is best to limit the number or to space their children. It is very important to note that the Catholic Church recognizes the validity of this decision.

The attempt to conceive or adopt a child should always be a joint decision of the wife and husband. A couple who easily agree with each other in these matters truly experiences a blessing. For many couples, however, there is usually a period of discussion about the issue as each one articulates his or her hopes and dreams. Then, loving agreements are made. It's always good advice to talk these things out and not to make assumptions about what your marriage partner thinks. The decisions to have a child, to space children, and to have no more children are certainly among the major ones of a marriage. That's why they should be done carefully, openly, honestly and prayerfully.

Once a plan of action has been agreed upon by a couple, then they must also exercise responsibility for choosing what method of birth control to use. The Catholic Church has been extremely clear on what it considers an essential element of the expression of sexual marital love: A couple is to be open to the creation of new life. In the most extensive treatment of this topic, Pope Paul VI said that marital love is productive ". . . for it is not exhausted by the communion between the husband and wife, but it is destined to continue raising up new life."

Belief in the value of new life is rooted in the conviction that life is ultimately from God. That is why the decision to parent does not only involve a couple's own preference but also the intent of God for them as they understand God's will. God does not place unbearable burdens on us but acts with us and through us for the best interests of all concerned.

TEACHING OF THE CHURCH

The teaching of the Catholic Church in opposition to the use of artificial methods of preventing conception is well known. The teaching is based on the inseparable purposes of marital sex: the development of the love between wife and husband and the creation of new life.

To quote the Second Vatican Council on this point: "Therefore, when there is question of harmonizing conjugal love with the responsible transmission of life, the moral aspect of any procedure does not solely depend on sincere intentions or on an evaluation of motives. It must be determined by objective standards. These, based on the nature of human persons and their acts, preserve the full sense of mutual life-giving and human procreation in the context of true love." In other words, when it comes to married love the Church teaches that you can't fully express your true love for each other without being open to creating new life.

Pope John Paul II has continued the teaching of this view and has added his own sensitivity to the procreative nature of married love. It is best to read his own words on this subject: "When a couple, by means of recourse to contraception, separate these two meanings that God the Creator has inscribed in the being of man and woman and in the dynamism of their sexual communion, they act as 'arbiters' of the divine plan and they 'manipulate' and degrade human sexuality and with it themselves and their married partner by altering its value of 'total self-giving.' Thus the innate language that expresses the reciprocal total self-giving of husband and wife is overlaid, through contraception, by an objectively contradictory language, namely, that of not giving oneself totally to the other. This leads not only to a positive refusal to be open to life, but also to a falsification of the inner truth of conjugal love, which is called upon to give itself in personal totality."

We have provided you with these quotes to emphasize that the foundation for the Church's view rests in a special understanding of the nature of marriage. It does not flow from a simple reading of the natural law but rather from a religiously informed human reading of the nature of marriage as a shared life of totality.

MORAL DECISION MAKING

It might be helpful here to review how Catholics are taught to make decisions in their moral life. While these principles apply to any question involving moral values, conscientious Catholics welcome them particularly when issues are quite complex or directly touch their personal lives.

Most of you have heard the phrase: "Follow your conscience." Some are surprised to learn that this notion comes directly from the center of the Church's teaching on morality. Where differences arise is in the understanding of what is meant by "conscience."

Conscience is not some alien little voice inside oneself that operates like a traffic light signaling "go," "stop," or "be careful." In fact, conscience is your own voice, which speaks when you are faced with options relating to free will. Traditional Catholic morality calls for us to first listen to and then adopt a Gospel perspective in making a moral decision by bringing to bear on one's thinking such values as love of neighbor, care for all life, respect for legitimate authority and honesty with oneself.

While some people intuitively recognize the right thing to do almost without thinking, others require a set of directions in making good moral decisions. To "follow one's conscience" according to Church teaching, you must begin by examining all the important aspects of the situation. In the context of birth control, you must look at personal motives (selfish or loving), evaluate the options available (abstinence, natural methods, artificial methods), and determine the consequences of different options (effect on your own body and your marriage relationship, effectiveness of the method). If you do this honestly in good faith and in light of the Church's teachings and the Gospel, only then can you make a decision for the good. That judgment of goodness is the judgment of an *informed* conscience. And it is *that* judgment one is obliged to follow.

NATURAL FAMILY PLANNING (NFP)

The use of NFP, the natural family planning method of birth control, respects the Church's teaching on marital love. It is in tune with the God of creation, who has designed the female human body in such a way that there are times of fertility and infertility. Should the couple decide that it is not the time for them to procreate a child, they engage in sexual relations only during the natural infertile periods of a woman's cycle. Likewise, if a couple wishes to conceive, they can plan their lovemaking to coincide with the woman's most fertile time.

There are many advantages to NFP. It is natural, highly effective, inexpensive, and medically safe. It is a method of birth control that is shared equally by husband and wife. NFP can foster spiritual, intellectual, emotional, and physical intimacy between a couple.

Practicing NFP requires daily observations and accurate record keeping to insure valid interpretation. Couples are invited to learn these methods from couples and individuals trained in the correct practice of this Church-approved method of family planning, classes in which are offered in most dioceses in the country.

INFERTILITY

If a couple is unable to have a child, it often seems that the desire to do so is all the greater. Infertility, a condition which seems to be growing each year, was once called "sterility." Better knowledge of the process of procreation, however, has brought us to be much less quick to label couples as sterile. True, some people are completely infertile (therefore "sterile"), but most couples are capable of having children with the help of modern medical procedures.

Exact statistics on the percentage of infertile married couples is not easily obtained, partly because some couples simply do whatever they can to prevent a pregnancy. In addition, everyone is aware of the tragically high number of abortions performed every year. But experts estimate that from ten to twenty percent of all couples experience some infertility, and that number is slowing increasing.

The causes of infertility are multiple, and each infertile couple may have some combination of factors unique to themselves. When the physical environment in an area is contaminated with destructive substances, for example, the reproductive rate is lessened. Given the toxic state of some of the air and water in our environment, it is not surprising that this may be part of the cause of infertility for some. The use of certain chemical fertility-control substances may also harm a woman's reproductive capabilities. The same can be said for abortion or the use of an interuterine device. Personal stress is also mentioned by some authorities as decreasing fertility in both men and women. Men can have physical problems that prevent sperm from maturing or impregnating an egg. Women can experience the inability to produce eggs or to deliver them to the uterus. And finally, attempting to have children at a later age can also restrict achieving a pregnancy.

The old myths which laid blame for infertility solely on the woman are simply false. The role of the male is also a factor.

If you desire children and fail to achieve your goal within a reasonable time—perhaps a year—consult with a medical fertility specialist. Help is available. You should feel no stigma or sense of inadequacy if you learn that you are infertile. While this situation can be a source of deep sadness and suffering, it can also bring the two of you closer together in your struggle to seek meaning and fulfillment in your marriage.

ADOPTION AND FOSTERING

Couples who are infertile, as well as fertile couples who would like to provide a family for infants or children without families, look to adoption as a way to express their love for each other and their generosity toward life. In the past, adoption was fairly easy. There were a good number of infants and children available. No longer is this the case. Widespread abortion, the use of birth control procedures, and the openness of society to single parents all have decreased the number of available adoptees. Some qualified couples wanting to adopt will have to wait many years.

In the last decade or so, a great deal of public attention has been focused on couples who have gone outside this country seeking to adopt infants and children from other lands. Often inThird World countries, where poverty and high birth rates are still the rule, there are orphanages quite willing to have their children adopted by parents from the United States. Many international organizations facilitate such adoptions. Some are under the sponsorship of churches.

In addition, special-needs children who are not easily adopted are often available. These children may bring certain physical or psychological challenges with them to a new family. Children who have experienced the horrors of abuse or neglect or who have been carried within their mothers while the mothers abused drugs or alcohol often have liabilities not shared by healthy babies. Part of the Christian way of life, however, includes the support and care of those with special needs. If you are one of those couples, either with or without children of your own, who feel called to make room in your family for one or more of these special children of God, you are indeed blessed.

Another option for couples wanting to care for children is foster care. Presently, there are about 400,000 children in the Unites States in foster care, with only a little over 100,000 families willing to care for them. In other words, there is a great need for foster families. Church and secular agencies oversee foster care, and they are ready and willing to talk with couples considering becoming foster parents. They can put you in touch with others like you who have taken on this needed ministry to the Lord's little ones. Of course, some of those in foster care are in their teens, so "little" might not be the best word for them! Nevertheless, they all remain children of God, and each deserves the best care possible.

While foster care and adoption may not be for everyone, it remains an important way for couples to express the love that is in their hearts. Those parents who already engage in either adoption or foster care will testify that it brings much more to them than they feel they give. Genuine Christian love, after all, is a paradox. The more you give, the more you receive in return.

FRUITFULNESS

Christian marriage is understood as a community of love between two spouses, and from their love new life is to be created and supported. Usually this takes the form of becoming parents of one's own biological children. We have also discussed the option of adoption or foster care. But even couples who, for a variety of valid reasons, do not have any children are still intended by God to be fruitful or, in other words, active in the service of life.

Many childless couples express their own fruitfulness by the effort they extend to help others outside their home. They may be volunteers in a homeless shelter, they may do extra tasks in their church community, or they might orient their entire married lives to doing what they can to make our world a better place.

Childless couples may be tempted to turn inward, to feel sorry for themselves, or to pursue a lifestyle of self-centeredness. While it is easily understood that theirs may be a deeply spiritual struggle to deal with their undesired childless marriage, nevertheless, as in all crises of life, they will be given God's help to accept and deal with their situation. Their marriage need not be any less fruitful than a marriage that produces a house full of kids.

FROM COUPLE TO FAMILY

The arrival of the first child is a moment of immense personal satisfaction and importance for a couple. It will also be "the moment that changed everything!"

Each marriage partner will have to adopt new roles. Each will begin to think and act in different ways. While both spouses may consider the new baby a most blessed event, there will inevitably be moments of anxiety joined with those of wonder.

Because of all this "newness," there is apt to creep into your relationship some misunderstanding and confusion. Typically, new moms devote almost all their time and attention to the baby. Occasionally, husbands feel like they have been replaced by a six-pound "intruder." As with all issues in marriage, it is important to talk about your feelings with each other. Discuss everything, because you will be establishing the "ground rules" for the next few years of your life together.

In the past, the tasks of infant care and child rearing were thought of mostly as the work of the mom. While old patterns pass away only slowly, today the task of parenting is recognized to fall equally on both the mom and the dad. That does not mean that they will always be doing exactly the same thing—or that they share everything fifty-fifty. Instead, the key is for both parents to see parenting as a shared experience, where the special gifts of the mom and the dad are offered to the new family members.

Certainly, the early weeks and months of parenting necessitate a change in your lifestyle and social life. Your family will now "enjoy" a big need, and that need is the baby. From all that we are learning about human development, the first year of life is very important and influences a child the rest of his or her life. It is most important that you create in your infant a feeling of reliability and trust. The world can be a scary place after spending all one's time in the cozy, warm environment of the womb, where all one's needs were fully taken care of. Being born is akin to taking a cold shower of reality. The infant feels natural fear and worry. Caring parents will know what's needed to comfort and communicate to their baby that this world really is a wonderful place to be, especially "in *our* family."

While it may seem that the little one takes all the time, energy and attention you have, it is also important that you take some "breathing time" and create some space for each of you alone and for the two of you together. A new baby does not have to be like a wedge between a new mom and dad. It can also bring you even closer together.

Think, too, about some of the very practical aspects of the momentous change associated with becoming a threesome (or more). Your notions of time, freedom, money and relationships with grandparents will undergo profound changes. None of these new factors have to be detrimental to your relationship. They just need to be noticed and dealt with. And speaking of the practical, it will not be long after the birth of a new baby that the issues of eating and sleeping become crises. This, too, will pass, but meanwhile it can severely disrupt your existing family patterns. Babies enter life with their own idea about meal times and bedtime. Rarely does it coincide with existing practice! As with all other aspects of infant care, share these tasks and responsibilities as equally as you can. And don't hold back from asking help from family and friends. Most people are quite willing to help, but they usually wait for an invitation from new parents.

Finally, both of you should enjoy the early days and weeks of the life of your new baby. They will pass quickly, and if you don't take the time to simply *be* with your baby, the time will fly by and you will wish you had done differently.

BLENDED FAMILIES

With divorce and single-parenting on the rise, we are also seeing a great increase in the number of so-called "blended families." A blended family is one which starts with one or both spouses already having children. It is sometimes referred to as a "yours, mine and ours" family.

A blended family will almost always have its special complexitles, mostly around the care of children. The parenting of stepchildren can create a high level of family stress. Making the situation even more complicated is the role of former spouses, grandparents and such mundane factors as inheritance, visitations and even issues surrounding heredity. Sometimes, too, there are problems between new siblings.

Again, the importance of honest and open communication in a family rises to the surface. Knowing right from the start that the creation of a blended family is *always* a major challenge will help as difficulties arise. Then, the expected tension and confusion will be recognized as no one's fault. It simply comes with the territory. Decrease of anxiety through understanding and patience will go a long way to making blended families work. In fact, they can grow to be strong, wonderful families where differences are accepted and even built upon. Nevertheless, it takes parents with large and generous hearts to make this happen.

PARENTING STYLES

In the ideal world, children are lovingly accepted and the whole family "lives happily ever after" their arrival. But in the real world, this is never automatic. Children can stretch and stress a marriage relationship, so it is important for a couple to establish some common understanding of how they will parent. This does not mean that they must have the same parenting style. In fact, there are experts who believe a little difference between mom and dad can enrich the life of a child. It "forces" children to deal with two types of authority. If the parents maintain exceedingly different approaches to parenting, however, the child can also become confused. So, as rules of thumb, keep the following points in mind:

* Never air serious differences in the presence of your children. It is certainly all right to disagree with each other, even in front of the children. But children become confused, and even scared, when parents "fight" with emotional intensity in their presence.

* Once you agree on a certain approach, remain consistent. Don't change the rules midway through the game. This can create serious anxiety in children. It also encourages them to be manipulative of a system which, from their perspective, seems to be rather loosely constructed.

* Don't try to "pass the buck," particularly in matters related to decision-making or discipline. Respond to children on the spot, and don't delay your reaction or give the impression that only one parent is the discipline person or the decision-maker.

* Take responsibility that is proper to parents. Don't depend on outside systems like the schools or the church or the police to do the work you should do. The family is the foundation for children's healthy development, and the parents are the master-builders.

In recent years, many fine publications have been written for parents. Parenting classes or workshops are often sponsored by church or local community groups. Talk with other experienced parents about what they have learned to make them more effective—and where they learned it.

Be careful about those approaches to parenting which assume that children are like wild animals that need to be tamed. For instance, no serious study of parenting has ever concluded that physical punishment or spanking of children is a very effective way of disciplining them. Given the widespread danger of child abuse, it is better to avoid violence of any kind within the family.

And finally, never, never, threaten abandonment as a punishment for misbehavior. We have learned that when a child thinks or actually experiences (even for a short time) abandonment by a parent, the child begins to think at a very deep level that something terrible "must be wrong with me." Threatened or actual withdrawal of parental affection or presence creates a climate in which shame or guilt can develop in the child.

The bottom line on parenting styles is for both of you to become informed, caring and patient parents. Everything else will work itself out. Remember, the role of loving parenthood is about as close we humans get to imitating the role of God in creation.

POINTS FOR REFLECTION

1. Parenthood will cost you time, money and energy, while at the same time it will make you a much better person. Parents raise children and children raise parents.

2. Because we all "age" each day, the task of parenting is constantly changing. Children grow from being totally dependent at birth to being semi-independent as young adults. Meanwhile, parents grow from the clumsy energy of young parents to the graceful wisdom of elders.

3. Children must become their own persons. Love them, support them, but don't attempt to "clone" them into a mirror image of yourself.

4. Children are part of the family, not the entire whole of it.

5. The best thing that parents can do for their children is to love each other.

QUESTIONS FOR DISCUSSION

1. Discuss with each other your hopes and fears concerning children in your marriage. Knowing that nothing is for certain, especially in this context, share with each other how many children you would like to have. How would you like them "spaced?"

2. Make a list of those qualities you already perceive in each other which would make you good parents.

3. There is a strong tendency in each person to parent as he or she was parented. Surface as much as you can about the positives and negatives each of you experienced from your parents. Discuss which tendencies or styles you wish to promote and which you would like to try to change.

One rainy Saturday afternoon, a father took on the task of keeping his ten-year-old daughter entertained. He tore a full-page map of the world out of a magazine, cut it into small pieces, and told her to tape it back together like a jig-saw puzzle.

To the father's amazement, the girl presented him with the completed puzzle in just a few minutes.

"How did you do it so fast?" the man asked.

"It was easy," his daughter answered. "At first when I tried to fit together all those little lines and dots and small print, it looked like an impossible job. But then I saw that there was a picture of a family on the other side of the map. Once I got the family together, the world took care of itself."

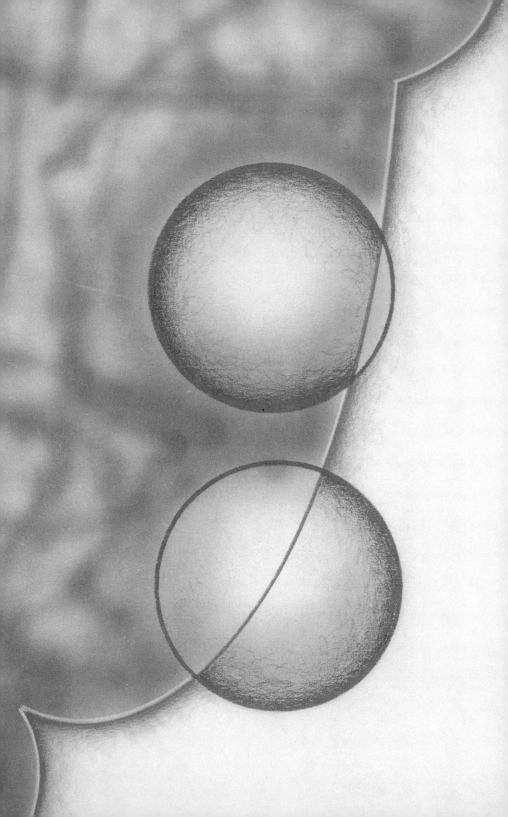

FINANCES

Money issues usually dominate national and state elections. Financial scandals are among the first to be discussed on the nightly news. Most people think about making, spending or investing money a good part of the day. It should, therefore, be of no surprise to learn that money is also one of the key factors in producing a happy or an unhappy marriage. You may be surprised to learn, however, that it is rarely the lack of adequate financial resources which destroys the happiness of a marriage. It is the couple's attitude toward material things.

Money not only buys cars and stereos and hamburgers and movie tickets, it also buys *power*. And it is always the power issue, more than the money issue itself, that wreaks havoc on a marriage.

A couple needs to reflect on what money means to each spouse. For some, it signifies security or the "worry free" life. For others, money means that the door of the store is open to buy, buy, buy. Some value money as freedom, a life of travel and adventure. A tip toward understanding yourself in this area: Usually we adopt the primary meaning we give to money from our parents. What were the attitudes of both your families of origin toward financial matters?

UNCERTAIN ECONOMIC FUTURE

In the times we now live in, most economists will predict only "modest gains" for the future. Given the world economic situation today, it is safe to conclude that the newly married may not even reach the economic level enjoyed by their parents. This scenario can easily create feelings of frustration, anger and even resentment.

To keep pace with this less than perfect economic situation, most couples now take it for granted that both wife and husband will need to have jobs. Two paycheck families are now the norm, rather than the exception they might have been just a few decades back. Along with having two jobs outside the home come problems like having adequate "time together," lack of sleep, housework which never seems finished, and—once children are a part of the family, or elderly relatives become ill—the need to care for the needs of dependents.

There is nothing essentially destructive about this vision of the economic future. It simply has to be added to the list of things requiring your attention if your marriage is to be deeply satisfying.

BLESSED FRUGALITY

A young reporter once met the aging John D. Rockefeller, who was sitting alone on a park bench. He asked, "Mr.

Rockefeller, how much is enough money?" The elderly tycoon pondered the question for a moment and then with a tight smile replied, "Just a little bit more, son. Just a little bit more."

Say the phrase "conspicuous consumption" five times very fast and you have said a mouthful. And that's part of what it means to be a conspicuous consumer. It seems that some time ago, someone must have made a very important observation. "If we produce only the goods and services people really need, we will soon run out of buyers for our products. And further, if we make things which never wear out, our market will soon evaporate." Thus began the attempt to influence consumers to buy more and more things that became obsolete as soon as they were paid for.

What has helped this movement immensely has been the growth of advertising. Whole industries are now supported by advertising, with television at the top of the list. It is estimated that a child growing up in today's world will have taken in almost *half a million* commercials by age eighteen—all with the same basic message: "Buy this and you will be happy." In more recent years, a new and refined strategy has been added. We are now being told that we all *deserve* certain things. This makes it seem almost a moral *obligation* to buy the product being offered.

Lastly, the producers of all the stuff that is now available to Mr. and Mrs. Consumer "promise" that using this or that product will enhance their identities. Wearing certain label clothes, drinking the right kind of beverage, or owning (or leasing = another ploy) the right set of wheels will bring them status and success.

Contradicting this whole conspicuous consumption approach is a growing number of individuals and couples who are saying "enough is enough." For these wise consumers, buying items that are durable and a true bargain is a basic value. Living simply and inexpensively is seen not only as a way to lessen the financial pressure on a family but also as a more spiritual way of life. Theirs is a move in the right direction. In marriage, the number one cause of strife and argument often has been around the use of money. Maybe you two will be part of the new movement toward blessed frugality.

ATTITUDES TOWARD MONEY

Money is one big and difficult context where differences in a marriage surface. Each partner brings separate attitudes toward money into a marriage. These range from who should earn the money (or most of it) to how it should be spent—and when.

Just as your backgrounds have influenced your attitudes toward sex, relationships and personal habits, so too do past experiences influence your feelings about money. Ed, who grew up in poverty and rarely had even the basic necessities of life, developed great insecurities about money. He needs a huge savings account, a piece of land, and an unmortgaged home to feel secure. Even minor expenditures on entertainment or frivolity are threatening to Ed. Judy, on the other hand, comes from a fairly affluent background and simply takes money for granted. She does not worry about where it comes from and might even spend it foolishly. The two of them had many arguments and misunderstandings in the first few years after their wedding. They finally agreed to give Judy a substantial amount of "mad money" each month to spend as she wanted but to budget the rest of their resources according to Ed's more conservative needs.

Another money issue concerns who "owns" or "controls" the money. This can be a special problem when one person brings more financial assets into a marriage or earns more than the other. Will full equality between the two of you be the primary value in all financial discussions? Or will one partner exercise authority while the other remains oblivious to your financial situation? Most couples fall somewhere in the middle, but rarely do wife and husband feel exactly the same.

No matter what your differing attitudes on money (and there will almost *certainly* be some differences), the important thing is that you learn to talk about your financial situation, come to some agreement on how you will handle it, and stick to your agreement.

TAKE INVENTORY

Many people enter marriage without a very developed understanding of money matters. Perhaps they were used to being supported by parents and were not personally responsible for their spending. Others, on the other hand, may have a nearly complete grasp of finances, which can be a very useful skill in the marriage.

Before you marry, sit down with your partner and list all the assets each of you is bringing to the marriage. List all your important possessions, including insurance policies, any stocks or bonds, savings accounts, investment accounts, etc. Next, list all your financial liabilities, for example unpaid college loans, money owed on a car, financial debts to parents, money owed on credit cards, and so forth. Be totally honest in these matters. If you have difficulty being straightforward with your future spouse, it may be a sign that you are not ready for marriage. Finally, move to the so-called bottom line and determine as exactly as you can your new family's financial "portrait."

Then, after you have done your premarital accounting, talk about your feelings and worries. A major source of personal stress and anxiety may focus on your economic future. There is nothing wrong with this, particularly if you are aware of your concerns and are willing to share them with your future wife or husband. A final suggestion is this: Try to take care of all your debts before your marriage. While this is not always possible, when it is done it starts the marriage off with a clean slate. It helps make the transition from "me" to "us" easier.

BUDGETING: A PROCESS AND A PLAN

Once you have come to a fairly close estimate of your joint worth, move to phase two of this exercise and make an estimate of the expenses you are likely to face in your first year of marriage. No couple can foresee all the unexpected expenses they will encounter, but even these unknowns can be covered by setting aside a savings account for emergencies.

Likewise, discuss how the two of you will handle the money affairs of your life. Who will pay the bills? Will you have a joint or separate checking account? What kind of credit cards will you have, and in whose name will they be listed?

Once you have estimated the costs for the basics like shelter, food, transportation, medical expenses, clothing and so forth, keep your figures for future use. You will have to make many adjustments in your plans. The primary reason for doing this exercise, however, is to make you as aware as possible of the movement of money in your married life. Starting out a home and a new life together can be expensive. It is all the more frightening when money moves around without your understanding. The growth of plastic money and automatic electronic transfers of funds can catch you unawares. Surprises can come in the mail at the end of the month when you receive an accounting of the month's "business."

It is a challenging enough enterprise to begin a new marriage without having to experience the stresses which come from poor money management. There are many books available to help you in your budgeting. Buy one and use it. Good money management in a marriage can be a very loving thing to do.

INSURANCE AND WILLS

Some of the hidden costs of a budget concern insurance. "Hidden" means that you do not usually receive something back upon payment. You are purchasing "security" against unforeseen mishap or illness, or even death. In our society, it is very dangerous for a family to live without basic insurance protecting their property, valuables, health and lives. Sometimes employers provide some insurance as part of their employee benefit packages, but there is a trend away from this. More and more, the burden of insurance expenses is falling on the individual or the family. Securing adequate insurance is another way of showing love. You do not want to risk the financial livelihood of those you love—especially your spouse and your children.

Wills are another area inviting your loving attention. Often people fail to realize that each state has a plan for the distribution of personal assets upon the death of any citizen without a will. It might be called the "generic will" for those who do not have a will. In some cases, the state's formula for passing on your assets will be exactly in accord with your wishes. It may not be, however, and that is why it is important for you to have a legally drawn up will that states precisely your desires. You might also want to consider signing a "living will" or a durable power of attorney that clearly states your desires regarding the administration of extraordinary medical procedures to prolong your life in situations in which you cannot make your own decision. All of this is mentioned so that the two of you will take that little extra effort needed to draw up instructions which correspond with what you want to happen. It is helpful to secure the assistance of an attorney to be sure that you do it right. An experienced attorney or financial counselor can also provide you with advice on other money matters related to your family situation.

CREDIT CARDS

The human race has traveled a long way from the time when the bartering of goods and services was the basic way people survived. Now it might be argued that we have gone to the opposite extreme, which is credit buying. In one sense, our economic system is based on credit. Most major purchases are "bought on time," which means that you pay for them over a long time and with substantial interest fees.

No two people approach credit buying with the same attitude. All credit buying involves some risk, and each person's tolerance for risk varies. Again, you can find excellent books on good approaches to home mortgages, car loans, etc. Learn as much as you can about the world of credit buying, because wise decisions can save thousands of dollars.

Credit cards have been the downfall of many couples. They are fairly easy to secure and their use seems so painless. You never actually *see* any money exchanged, so the reality of spending hard-earned dollars is blurred by simply signing a receipt. Too many consumers have overspent their resources and have been buried by excessive charging of purchases. The effect of this kind of irresponsibility on a marriage can be devastating. One of the most destructive postures toward one's spouse is blaming. Yet, it is blame that quickly rises to the surface when a couple learns that one or both of them has been "fast and loose" with the "plastic."

Appealing to the dreams of consumers is what our economic system thrives on. We are advised by commercials that our unhappiness, our pain and suffering, our insecurity and lack of popularity will be taken care of if we just buy product x, y or z. So in weaker moments, we do just that. The solution is an honest awareness of what's happening in your daily financial life. Credit cards are not evil in themselves, but they can be easily abused, and you will be the ones who suffer in the end.

WISE USE OF MONEY

While it would be a clear distortion of Christian values to consider money as the most important thing in life, it does have an important role. Money can be used in the service of your health, your happiness, your ability to give help to others, and your ability to insure a better future for you and those who depend upon you. Careful attention to all the details of your life, which include money, expresses your fundamental values. While an excessive concern for money can imply a distortion of your values, it is equally destructive to be totally indifferent to finances. Virtue lies—as usual—between the extremes. See what you can do to drop finances from their long standing number one position as a source of marital conflict and to make them instead one of the building blocks of your successful family.

POINTS FOR REFLECTION

1. Keeping up with the Joneses can be a very counterproductive endeavor.

2. It is always better to decide where your money will go than wonder where it went.

3. Spending or saving can be as much a personal addiction as alcohol, drugs and gambling.

4. There is nothing sadder for a couple to discover than that they have increased their wealth or social prestige at the cost of their relationship.

5. If you both die in a car crash on your honeymoon, who will get all your stuff?

QUESTIONS FOR DISCUSSION

1. Discuss with each other any problems your parents had with money. How was money talked about in your family?

2. What is your plan for having some kind of a budget in the first year of marriage? What schedule will you adopt for reevaluating and revising it?

3. Do you plan to change the splending habits of the person you are about to marry? If so, discuss your plans now.

You are possessed by the things you possess. They claim your time and effort in paying for them; they sap your emotional and physical energy in worrying about them, protecting them, caring for them; they fill your imagination with dreams of how to get more of them.

The first fruit of poverty of spirit,

of detachment,

of schooling yourself in not wanting more things, is freedom.

If you are truly in love, your love for each other will want to burst out of your relationship—like new wine in old wineskins. You will want to give, not take. The best gift you can give is yourselves— your time, your interest, your talents—to projects, to works of compassion, to worthy causes. Nor can you ignore your treasure (however meager it may be at the moment)! If you are truly thankful for the blessing of your love, you will want to share your possessions with those less fortunate than you.

Give as if your marriage depended on it.

It does.

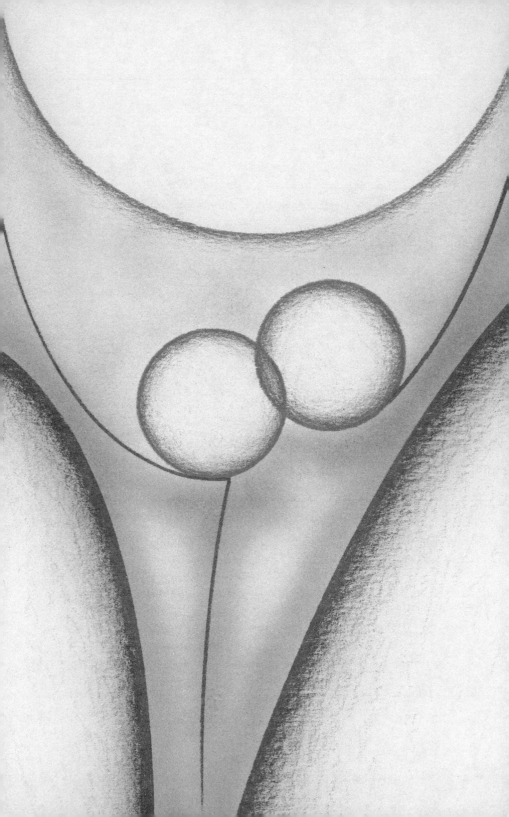

Marriage in Christ

Throughout this book, we have repeated over and over again that the creation of a healthy and happy marriage is no easy task. It requires self-understanding, awareness of each other, an appreciation and acceptance of the differences between women and men, and finally a love that is as deep and as broad as the oceans. You will find help from family and friends on your journey together, but for the most part you will be on your own.

Yet there is one other person who is deeply interested in you and your marriage. God, who made each married couple so wonderfully unique, is also there to support them in good times and bad times. Jesus promised as much when he promised to send the Holy Spirit to be with us always.

LOVE OF JESUS

Love is never boastful, nor conceited, nor rude;
never selfish, nor quick to take offense.
Love keeps no score of wrongs; does not gloat
over other's sins, but delights in the truth.
There is nothing that love cannot face; there is no
limit to its faith, its hopes, and its endurance.
Love will never come to an end. In a word,
there are three things that last forever: faith,
hope and love; but the greatest of them all is
love.

I Corinthians 13

Loving is never easy. In fact, it is among the most difficult of all human acts. We learn about love from observing others and by being loved by others.

Maybe you have never thought of this before, but the greatest human lover of all time was the carpenter's son, Jesus of Nazareth. Everyone can learn about love from his example. Everyone can be comforted by his love for each of us.

God so loved the world and each person in the world that the divine became flesh in Jesus Christ—the Anointed One. This is the foundation of the Christian faith: Jesus taught us how to live a fully human life and how to love one another as God loves us.

A husband and wife can look to the love of Jesus as a model of love that is life-giving in the fullest possible way. Jesus, of course, was not married, but his love for others was total. It was at maximum level all the time. In John's Gospel, we read that during the Last Supper Jesus summed up his life in these terms: "This is my commandment; love one another as I have loved you." These words could be the motto for every married couple.

COMMUNITY OF LOVERS

There are many ways to describe the Church, which is made up of the disciples of Jesus throughout history and today. Perhaps the best description is that the Church is the community of those who try to love as did Jesus.

This kind of love "explains" how couples can pledge to stay together for a lifetime "no matter what." It explains how parents can care for their children with patience and understanding, without considering the cost.

The Church is a community of people who try to love in extraordinary ways. The Church is not perfect, nor is its love. Vatican II speaks of the Church as being on a "pilgrimage," which means that it has not yet arrived at perfection. Part of the challenge of being a Christian is accepting the invitation to greatness while at the same time knowing that one is not great. In the Christian life, vision blends with reality to equal struggle. For married couples, part of this struggle is to be faithful to their marriage vows.

SACRAMENTS

Sometimes the loving power of God meets the receptive openness of Christian believers with powerful results. When this cooperative moment happens publicly, in formal rituals marked by words of faith and love, we say that God becomes "sacramentally" present.

Historically, the Catholic Church has identified seven rituals having this sacramental meaning. The seven sacraments of the Church are associated with major moments or events in human life. At these times, Christians try to open themselves to God's presence in a special way, so that the "recipients" of the sacraments—as well as the whole Church—are transformed by God's loving power. It took more than one thousand years for the Church to officially name the seven sacraments. The last to receive that designation was the sacrament of marriage or matrimony. (The others are baptism, confirmation, the eucharist, reconciliation, holy orders, and the anointing of the sick.)

As a sacrament, Christian marriage has two special features that differentiate it from the other six.

* The sacrament of marriage is actually conferred by each spouse on the other. The official witness, which is usually a priest (although exceptions can be made), is simply a witness to the activity taking place *between* the two spouses coming-to-be.

* Due to the ongoing nature of Christian marriage, the wife and husband remain "givers of the sacrament" throughout their lives. By carrying out their vows, they continue to administer the sacrament to each other. Marriage is truly "the gift that keeps on giving."

SYMBOLS

Human beings create symbols as a way to carve out meaning from the world of chaos. All language is nothing more than a set of organized symbols. The wedding ceremony and celebration are filled with symbols. The bride and groom usually give to each other rings in the shape of a circle, symbolizing that they hope that their love will be without end. Flowers are often a part of the wedding celebration, symbolizing the abundance of creation. Different ethnic groups have special music, dances or foods, all of which indicate that a wedding is something special.

In the Catholic Church, the sacraments are symbols of God's presence and interaction with the gathered community. The symbols indicate the coming together of something from God and something from humans. In a sense, each sacrament is a meeting, an encounter, between God and God's people. Learning about sacramental symbolism helps us grasp the deeper meaning of what is taking place.

To help people develop appropriate attitudes and dispositions, the Church uses art, language, music and ritual to awaken the response of the gathered. Sacraments are like calls in the night darkness. They come to drag us from sleep and lethargy. They are designed to excite all those who are present. Often they fail, but this is not the "fault" of the sacrament. They remain as invitations to awaken to God's presence.

SACRAMENTAL COUPLES

If Jesus had not come to transform humankind into a new creation, marriage would still be a holy and blessed union. It would not, however, have been raised to a new level of meaning, one which symbolizes the very love of God for us and the totally generous love of Jesus for his Church.

When the wife and husband, conscious of the deep love of Jesus for them, seek to freely manifest the same kind of love for each other, we say that they have achieved a "sacramental marriage." Their love is faithful and exclusive, and they intend their love to be fruitful by remaining open to the creation of new life through their sexual love.

The couple is graced or empowered by God to make such a magnificent statement of love. The sacrament of matrimony brings them to a deeper level of the possibilities of love. They, in turn, become symbols to the rest of the Church, and to society, that love of immense proportions is truly possible and that God can do great things through us, if we are sufficiently open to God's power.

SACRAMENT TO EACH OTHER

A church wedding means more than having the ceremony in a dignified or fancy place. It is intended to communicate something about the history of the couple and their belief that the deepest power in the world comes from God's love. In other words, the exchange of marital promises or vows is not just for the benefit of the couple, but is announced publicly before God and the community as a sacred statement of the couple's intent to live their entire lives together in God's presence.

The focus of the ceremony is on the couple and their free and public affirmation of their desire to be married to each other "in good times and in bad times, in sickness and in health, until death do them part." They are joined, bonded, yoked together for life, even though they are actually unsure about their future as they make their promises.

It is important for you to "preview" your wedding liturgy so that you can be familiar with its language and symbols. After all, they are designed for you to make the ceremony your own.

In many cases, couples even write their own vows. Only the basic Christian understanding of marriage needs to be respected in creating them. For in Christian marriage, it is the two of you—not the Church, not your family and friends—who are the sacrament to each other. What matters is not so much what you *say* to each other as what you *do* with and for each other for the next, hopefully, fifty or so years.

SACRAMENT TO THE WORLD

The sacraments of the Church, while from God, are created for humans. The waters of baptism remind us of eternal life. The oil of the anointing of the sick reminds us that God is a God of healing. In Christian marriage, the "reminder" of the sanctity of married life is the married couple themselves.

In a world that has grown quite complacent about marriage, Christians cannot accept the flippant view. (If it works out, fine. If it doesn't, that's OK, too.) Marriage is serious business. Granted, some marriages fail. Human frailty can frustrate the best of intentions. Nevertheless, the Christian perspective on marriage is that it is part of God's wondrous plan.

Let's just say that there is a special *conviction* about marriage in the Church. It is an attitude of willingness to invest one's full strength in developing a love relationship that will last a lifetime. This love will spill over from the married couple to their future children, to the rest of their family, and to the whole wide world. The Christian vision of marriage includes a grand picture of life in general and the incredible possibilities that can occur between a couple when they are filled with love.

MARITAL SPIRITUALITY

"Spirituality" is a word used to describe how your spirit and God's spirit join in the everyday realities of your life. Spirituality focuses on how you use your time and energy. It is especially about how you love.

Traditionally, the topic of spirituality concerned only those aspects of life which were considered "religious." Spirituality was limited to personal prayer and participation in the sacred worship of the local church.

While it does not undermine the important religious practices mentioned above, spirituality in marriage also includes the daily events of married life. The spiritual acts of marriage include every act of generous love between wife and husband. This means anything (from a married couple's sexual encounters to their doing the dishes together to one or both of them going out to make a living for their family) is an important part of marital spirituality.

Developing a loving marriage relationship requires discipline and sacrifice. This does not mean that one partner need take on the role of martyr. In fact, always giving in to one's spouse can be a sign of unhealthy love. In marriage, there ought to be deep respect for the individuality of the other on the part of both the wife and the husband. Maintaining radical equality is part of marital spirituality.

Each person will bring to the marriage his or her personal spirituality, but part of marital spirituality is being open to the spiritual insights and behavior of one's marriage partner. There is only one God, and that God wills that marriage bring spouses closer together. Spirituality should not be a force which divides but rather a power and a presence which joins a couple ever more deeply to each other.

Therefore, it is important for each of you to communicate to the other your own personal spiritual journey. Your response to your partner's revelations should be one of wonder and respect, never judgment, rebuke or hostility.

You are standing at the starting line, positioning yourself for one of the great adventures of your life. Your marriage has the power not only to announce that you love each other but also that God can be "seen" in your love. If your marriage is truly "in Christ," you will come to know experientially that "those who abide in love abide in God, and God in them."

POINTS FOR REFLECTION

1. Your marriage will now be the primary way you fulfill your baptismal vows.

2. The support for a married couple by others is all the more important today because of the forces in society which don't really care whether or not a marriage succeeds.

3. Your Christian faith does not exempt you from the ordinary challenges of marriage but rather calls you to even greater effort and commitment.

4. The sacrament of your marriage will be a visible symbol to others of God's faithful and forgiving love.

5. Although people experience life only as individuals, they can maintain life only in organized groups. The same is true for married couples. Will the two of you join a church together after you are married?

QUESTIONS FOR DISCUSSION

1. Why do *you* want a church wedding?

2. If you ran into trouble in your marriage, to whom would you first turn? What kind of support might you seek from your church?

3. Describe your personal spiritual life to each other. Are there any elements of it that you would like to share with your partner after you are married?

Come, my lover, let us go forth

to the fields

and spend the night among the

villages.

Let us go early to the vineyards,

and see

if the vines are in bloom,

If the buds have opened,

if the pomegranates have

blossomed;

There I will give you my love.

The Song of Songs

TWO FAITHS, ONE LOVE

One of the major themes of this book Is that marriage involves the joining of two persons who are as different from each other as night and day. Male and female God created them . . . and then the fun began!

The first task of marriage for a couple is accepting, understanding and dealing with the basic differences between a woman and a man with respect and love.

The next level of differences concerns each partner's family and ethnic background. The differences encountered here can be quite profound or, if both partners come from similar backgrounds, the struggle to accommodate may be less difficult.

The final major set of differences that affects virtually every marriage revolves around religious beliefs and practices. Just because a couple both may have been raised Catholic—or Protestant or Jewish or Muslim, for that matter—does not mean that their religious faith, as it exists on the personal level, is exactly the same in both of them.

OLD ATTITUDES

What follows can be applied to the religious situation in all marriages, although it is particularly important in marriages where the couple come from different religious traditions, or when one partner professes no religious belief.

In the past, when two people from different religious backgrounds married, it signaled big trouble ahead. It was assumed that, in matters of religion at least, the couple would have nothing in common. The best hope for them was for each partner to simply practice his or her religion privately. Certainly they were never to discuss religion, as it would easily lead to arguments. This strategy opted for silent, peaceful co-existence. Such marriages were described as "mixed," and there was a time when these weddings could not even be celebrated in the sanctuary of a Catholic church.

We have traveled a long way from those "dark ages." Yet, occasionally, you can run across these old attitudes in both clergy and laity who are uninformed of the Church's present teaching on this issue.

Today's approach is to accept the religious differences of the two spouses and to try to maintain a positive attitude about their different beliefs and practices. We now speak of "interfaith" marriages and put the emphasis on the positive aspects of joining two faiths in one love.

CULTURAL DIFFERENCES

Culture has been described as our "second skin." It includes *everything* we have learned about how to live life. All our language, our social habits, even some of our facial expressions, are rooted in our culture.

One of the best ways to gain an awareness of the broad nature of culture is to travel in a country not yours by origin and to really try to live like those whose home it is. Dress the way they do, eat their foods, and try to take on as much as you can that is local. Eventually, you will realize that you are being challenged to change not merely some things but just about everything.

This experience can sometimes lead people to reject the other culture completely. They seem to conclude that the best way to maintain their own ways is to put down those of others.

In a marriage, it is important for a couple to recognize that, basically, they each come from a different culture. (This is true to some extent even when both people come from remarkably similar backgrounds.) As they face each other's cultural differences, couples need to be aware of the tendency to put down different ways to protect one's own. Like the good traveler in another country, they need to "go native" for a while and try to appreciate the new culture they have just "married into."

In other words, married couples must accept the fact that there are more than one way to do things. They must learn from each other different ways to celebrate holidays, educate children, deal with neighbors or in-laws, even (here's a *big* difference in some marriages) to clean house. Unfortunately, almost everyone who attempts marriage becomes critical at some point of his or her spouse's ways of doing things—that is, of his or her culture.

RELIGION AND CULTURE

The influence of culture is very powerful, and religion is one of the core elements. Religious tradition tells people the basic meaning of life—how it began; how it will end; what they must do to live well; how to put themselves in touch with God; and how to handle love, sex, guilt and death. Religion often gives us our very names. It gives us a vocabulary (sin, love, forgiveness, redemption), and provides powerful symbols (the Cross, the Star of David, Mecca) that shape our deepest thoughts. Religion tells us of sacred places and sacred times of the year and gives special form to our lives and personalities. A person does not give up this entire meaning system, or even modify it substantially, without feeling a sense of anxiety and loss.

But at the same time, it must also be acknowledged that many religions are quite similar. Usually, most religious differences are over nonessential aspects. These "trappings" of religion can change—and many of them have.

For example, some people at the time of Vatican II opposed the change of the language of the Mass from Latin to English. Occasionally, one heard the argument that the words said by Jesus when he instituted the eucharist could not be altered. As a matter of fact, Jesus spoke a language called Aramaic, and he never used Latin. The argument was over religion, but it was not about what is really central to the Catholic faith.

The point is this: Religious differences are important, but how we respond to them is also important. In accepting these differences, a couple can find a precious opportunity for growth and a deepening of the understanding of what each other's culture is about. Differences are not necessarily problems. They can be opportunities.

One strategy for a marriage of mixed religious background is to simply consolidate the couple's two faiths and create a new religion. A little of this and a little of that and everyone will be happy. Right?

The problem with this approach is that religion is not just some set of ideas or beliefs, with a few rituals added. Religion is a way of living that is centered in its followers. There is a certain integrity to every particular religious tradition.

MUTUAL UNLOCKING

It is obviously important for an interfaith couple to learn about each other's religious tradition. More than book knowledge is important, however. If you are in this situation, you need to visit each other's churches or places of worship, enter the ceremonies as much as you are comfortable, meet members of the two religious groups, talk to other couples who face similar challenges, and have the courage to seriously consider "the truth" of the other tradition.

As this process of "mutual unlocking" unfolds, both of you will most likely feel, at times, that you are walking on thin ice. Often our personal religious beliefs are on shaky ground, but, because they tend to play only a small role in our thinking and acting, our shallowness is not noticed. But in the process of explaining our faith to others, our ignorance becomes obvious—even to ourselves. In other words, we may be somewhat religiously illiterate about our own faith.

Working through the conversation of your religious differences, however, can stimulate your learning about your own faith. The attempt to be clear to your partner may reveal how muddy your own understanding may be. It might be helpful for both of you to take part in classes or conversations for adults on each of your religious traditions.

Sometimes you can study each other's religion for the purpose of understanding it, only to return to your own faith more committed. Or, you may both decide that one of your two religious faiths makes the most sense for both of you. The key is not to be defensive but to search together for what is best for you as individuals and for your marriage.

DIFFERENCES ARE REAL

Communication can be both tricky and fun. Perceptions are equally as precarious a game. Did you ever play "the telephone game?" That's when one person whispers something to another and the message is passed around the group. The last person then tells what, supposedly, the first person had said. Rarely has the message retained its integrity.

Theorists in the field of communication tell us that our perceptions are all influenced by our preexisting personal state. Everyone "hears" in light of past experience. The message gets amplified or modified as it is passed on.

Something similar happens in the passing on of a religious tradition. Some is remembered correctly, and some is distorted. All of us, no matter what our personal religious background, have our own personal version of our religions. No two Catholics are exactly alike, nor are any two Buddhists. It is helpful to reflect on this, because that allows us to be more tolerant of differences between people. Religion can take a tenacious hold on people and make them very stubborn and self-righteous. Their religious posture lacks an essential feature of holiness: humility. Only God knows it all. We all come in a distant second.

It is always difficult to provide general rules for dealing with religious differences. Some people grow up with a seemingly inexhaustable reservoir of tolerance, empathy and understanding, while others are as rigid as an iron pole. Some families encourage acceptance, while others foster judgment. In a marriage, the key to success is not the absence of differences—they will always be there to some degree—but how you deal with them in a manner that strengthens the marriage. Part of the solution is good listening skills and a willingness to learn from each other.

THE UNINTERESTED

Often one partner is a committed religious believer, while the other is more or less disinterested. This can create a problem if the religious person takes on the challenge, or even the responsibility, of converting the other spouse to his or her religious orientation. The religious rhetoric of some groups encourages this process. It is one thing to simply offer to share your beliefs and values with your partner and quite another to attempt to force acceptance of your religion by the other.

Vatican II promulgated the principle of religious freedom, which included the notion that religion is so important and so personal that it should be offered and accepted only in freedom. Manipulation of your partner on religious matters is, therefore, out of line. If your partner is disinterested in religion, you can pray for him or her, you can show by example how important religion is to you, but you may not try to force a change.

THE INTERESTED

Stu is a Methodist and Maria is a Catholic. He went regularly to Sunday school and she attended a Catholic school for several years. They each go to each other's churches often, and they have begun to learn about each other's religious traditions. They both believe in God and in the central importance of Jesus in their daily lives.

Their future marriage offers them a tremendous opportunity to allow each of their faith traditions to enrich the other. Some call their situation "grassroots ecumenism."

As the years pass, Stu and Maria will continue to explore what they each hold important in their respective faiths. At some future time, one of them may decide to explore the possibilities of joining the other's church. This should be approached very carefully. No pressure should enter into the decision.

It is helpful to know that research shows that two people who each have strong religious faith, whether they be of the same religion or not, experience the best likelihood of building a successful marriage. Implied in this finding, of course, is that the couple approach religious faith as a force which brings them closer together rather than divides them.

THE FERVENT VERSUS THE TEPID

Sara attends her synagogue regularly and is strongly committed to her Jewish tradition. Tony was baptized a Catholic, but after he received the sacrament of confirmation the practice of his faith decreased to almost nothing. He still believes in God, prays occasionally, but no longer attends Mass. Sara and Tony share many common interests, but religion is not one of them. You might say that they have a "mixed marriage" from the standpoint of religious fervor, with one being committed and the other detached.

If you are the fervent member, consider the following:

* Discuss with your partner his or her personal religious history. Why did he or she lose interest in religion? Has there ever been any thought about returning to the practice of faith? The goal of your discussion is not to change anything, but simply to gain a clear understanding of your spouse's religious feelings.

* Above all else, do not try to force your own convictions upon your partner. Religious faith must always grow in an environment of freedom.

* Make sure that the lack of religious commitment of the person you hope to marry will not be a major burden for you. If you suspect it will, it may be a reason to reconsider whether you should marry that person. This can be a very painful matter, but you should be as honest as possible about it.

If you are the less religiously oriented partner, consider the following:

* Try to understand how important religion is to your future spouse. Be sensitive and don't ridicule his or her convictions. The best approach is one of respect.

* Do you have any hope that your spouse will drop his or her religious beliefs and practices after you are wed? If this is in your mind, be loving enough to discuss it honestly with your partner now.

* At least try to be open to learning the basics of your partner's religion. If it is an important part of his or her life, you owe it to both of you to understand, and even appreciate, what makes it so.

THE INVOLVED (OR OVERINVOLVED)

In this group are those couples who are both very deeply committed to their religion, whether it is the same faith or different. One thing we know about deep religious involvement is that it can become a very powerful force in one's life.

In marriage, religious faith can add tremendous energy to the relationship. It can assist a couple over the trying or hard times. It can also add excitement to the good times. It always provides deep meaning to their marital and family experience.

We all know, however, that religious commitment can be overdone. While this is certainly not always (or even usually) the case when a couple are both fervent believers, fanaticism is a danger they must be aware of and avoid.

RELIGIOUS TOLERANCE

Earlier, we mentioned how "mixed marriages" are really an opportunity to build a productive "interfaith" marriage.

If you stand back and reflect on religions in general, you will probably conclude that almost all of them are basically oriented to developing a relationship between their followers and the true God, however they imagine God to be. Different traditions have different names for that God. The characteristics of God, how God is involved in this world, and how God "feels" about us varies from tradition to tradition. Nevertheless, we have to assume that, deep down, all people of good will are seeking the same God.

This fact can serve as the basis for a common religious orientation in a marriage in which the couple does not share a common religious tradition. First, they must affirm that which is believed in common. Second, they must acknowledge those things which are different and try to determine whether, in those differences, there may be some commonality.

Some say we live in a "postmodern" world. One of the major aspects of this world is the acceptance of diversity. The recognition of the positive aspects of differences between people does not mean that there is no objective truth in the world but rather that truth can be approached from many perspectives. Further, each perspective is capable of discovering truths which other perspectives may not notice.

Tolerance may seem like a wishy-washy word, but at its heart is a respect for other people. We suspend harsh judgment toward them. We allow them to be as they are. We know that we can *never* know exactly what goes on inside another person. Thus, religious tolerance is a good foundation for approaching any differences which happen to exist between wife and husband in a marriage.

PRACTICAL APPROACH

What follows are some practical suggestions for allowing religious differences to strengthen your marriage.

* Encourage each other to be faithful to his or

her personal religious convictions and practice of faith.

* Attend each other's religious activities occasionally. When your partner's church or synagogue or mosque offers educational or ministerial opportunities, get involved in them together.

* Try to get to know some of the other members of your spouse's religious community as mutual friends.

* Become involved in the social and recreational opportunities offered by each other's faith communities.

* Deal early in your marriage with the practicalities of the religious practice of your spouse. Know that he or she will be attending scheduled activities and adjust your common schedule accordingly.

* Perhaps there are spiritual disciplines that you can develop in common. One example would be to learn to pray together in a way that is comfortable for both of you.

* Think of how religious activities can be woven into the activities of your home. For instance, the celebration of Thanksgiving can be a wonderful opportunity to blend religious traditions.

* Consider subscribing to different religious publications and read books in common about religious matters. And be sure to discuss them with each other.

* Find one common charitable religious activity which you will do in common. It might be a special project to assist the poor and homeless or something to do with children or the elderly.

CATHOLIC INTERFAITH PROCEDURES

Following the Second Vatican Council, the Catholic Church established procedures for Catholics marrying non-Catholics that are more open and respectful. There are certain legal aspects of interfaith marriage which you will need to consider, however. These will all be explained to you by your local parish staff.

For example, the Catholic Church still hopes (in general) that Catholics will marry Catholics. So when one is marrying a non-Catholic, certain "permissions" are to be sought. These are readily given, but it is something that has to be done. The involvement of the non-Catholic in these legal procedures is designed to help both parties understand what's expected of the Catholic partner from the standpoint of his or her own Church.

At an earlier time, non-Catholics were asked to promise certain things—for example, that they would allow the children to be raised in the Catholic Church. This no longer applies. The non-Catholic is not asked to promise anything. Catholic partners, however, are asked to do "all in their power" to see that children are raised Catholic. Note the wording, because this is not an absolute promise. One's power is obviously limited by the condition of the marriage and by the fact that children are also the children of the non-Catholic parent. Nevertheless, the Church would like to have the children raised Catholic (if it didn't, the Church would be totally indifferent to its own mission). But the Church also knows that the rights and responsibilities of the non-Catholic partner are part of the equation as well.

Specific requirements about the wedding—who can participate, whether the marriage can take place in the church of the non-Catholic, and a whole host of other issues—are best discussed with your local parish staff. Different dioceses may have slightly different regulations, so it is important to ask. The Church wants to have a positive and supportive attitude toward your marriage, and it will try to do all it can to make your wedding one that is holy and memorable.

FAMILIES

Your families' attitudes towards your interfaith marriage may depend on your parents' ages and on your ages; on how deeply they are committed to and involved in their faith tradition; on their general openness to new ideas; on how much maturity and responsibility you have acquired and displayed; on whether you are an only child or have siblings; on whether there have been other interfaith marriages in the family; etc.

Some engaged couples have the simple task of informing their families. Others may have some explaining to do. Still others may have to reconcile their families to an idea the families find hard to accept. A few may sadly decide to proceed without their family's full consent.

Remember, family is important. Be careful of thinking, "We are marrying each other, not each other's families." This is not completely true. You cannot write off family that easily. You have lived in great intimacy with mother, father, brothers and sisters for many years. For a long time, your self-image and self-esteem depended on their understanding, support and approval. Family means roots, belonging and community. Family is part of your bone and being.

Some people are totally free spirits. They can live away from family easily and can even tolerate their disapproval. Few of us, however, can do this without some anxiety and regret. No matter how certain you feel right now that you will never again need anyone except each other, please believe that this will pass. You will experience joys so great that you will want to share them with special people who care—bringing your newborn child to your mother and father; showing them your apartment or new car. Remember, sorrows will come, as will pain and worry. The comforting presence of family, people who are loving and concerned, can mean a great deal. Resolve now to take the trouble to be thoughtful and diplomatic with both your families in the weeks before the wedding. They are worth the investment.

Try to understand and work with your family's feelings. Some parents will be worried that their child may change or abandon his or her religion. This feeling may be mixed with a certain amount of guilt or uneasiness: "Where have we failed in passing on our beliefs?" Some parents may fear you will face stress and discord or that your religious differences may not provide the firm foundation and sustaining power that their common faith gave them. Still other parents—let's face it—might be chiefly concerned about what relatives, friends, neighbors and clergy might think.

All of these are, more or less, legitimate concerns. How do you work with them? Well, you certainly don't make points by implying that parents are "old-fashioned," intolerant or uninformed. Don't threaten their deeply held and cherished convictions. Show that you understand their anxieties and reassure them that neither of you have dismissed God and religion from your lives.

Help them to get to know your partner. This is one of the most positive and constructive moves you can make. The very qualities that attracted you to your beloved will almost certainly be appreciated by your families, too. The process requires some patience and the investment of time. As strangeness recedes and bonds are discovered, the personality of your fiance will come to the fore and the labels—"that Catholic boy," "that Moslem girl"—will fade away. Sometimes one relative is more open to the idea than the others. Enlist his or her aid to break ground with the rest of the family.

Many parents have no objections to interfaith marriages. They know you and trust your judgment and maturity. But even they may need help to understand wedding plans and religious customs and practices that are unfamiliar to them. A good briefing that answers their questions can be very helpful.

CHILDREN

In matters of religion, especially if the parents are from different faiths, children need special sensitivity and respect. Children enter the world without any religious faith. They learn about God from both their mother and their father, even if the parents are unaware of it. Children are like sponges. They observe and make judgments about what is important. Some claim that young children even think of their parents as gods! (Don't worry, this belief dies quickly.)

It is important not to raise a child in a religious vacuum. If wife and husband have different religious orientations, both views should be communicated to their children. Earlier we stressed the importance of discovering all that you have in common in the religious sphere. Share that information very strongly with your children. Don't allow your children to develop the view that you are deeply divided, especially in a matter of such great importance. Such a perception will deeply confuse them.

Another common error is to let children decide about religion when they are "old enough." Until then, these parents teach nothing about either of their religious beliefs or practices. The problem here is that, as was already noted, children are always learning, whether you intend it or not. In this case, they are learning that religion is not important to either of their parents. So answer your children's questions and share with them your separate views of God, prayer, values, morality and the meaning of life. Like all of us, children will learn part and forget part of what they are taught, and they will eventually grow up to put together their own personal religious understanding. You both will contribute, but neither of you will have the final word.

MODEL OF MARITAL UNITY

The interfaith couple stands in a special place in this world. Historically, religion has been used as the excuse for wars, riots and persecution—all in the name of God. But this has been a terrible misuse of religion.

True religious faith is an attempt to get to the heart of human existence and in that process to bring people closer together in mutual service, respect and love. In a marriage where there exist two distinct faiths, that marriage can show that love can conquer all differences. Two faiths can become one love!

POINTS FOR REFLECTION

1. Although many interfaith couples will be aware of and resist biases or prejudices, their relatives and friends may not.

2. It is sometimes better to admit that some beliefs and practices will remain "nonnegotiable" and work on those which may be shared in common.

3. Some interfaith couples have to hold their ground against well-meaning family members or even fellow church members. Remember, the two of you, in harmony with God, are in charge of your own religious lives.

4. People indifferent or antagonistic to religion on the surface may have many serious unresolved religious conflicts within themselves.

5. The Catholic approach to interfaith marriages may appear one-sided, but the Church is truly concerned about your having a good marriage and will support you to that end.

QUESTIONS FOR DISCUSSION

1. What are those parts of your own religious beliefs and practices which are most important to you? Share these with your partner.

2. What are the positive religious features of your relationship that you hope to develop after you marry?

3. Discuss and agree now upon the religious education of your children. Write the agreement down and review and revise it when each child is born, gets old enough to be taken to religious services, and begins school.

May your marriage be a
long adventure in personal growth

May you have true friends to stand
by you in joy and in sorrow

May you be deeply involved in
the events of your times

May you take time to reflect
on the wonder of being

May you see you children's
children to the third and
fourth generation

May you come to old age and
gray hair in peace and
contentment

May you be kind to each other always